CONNECTIONS

"Only connect."

—E. M. FORSTER

The interpreter's subject consists "ever, obviously, of the related state, to each other, of certain figures and things. To exhibit these relations, once they have been recognized, is to 'treat' his idea, which involves neglecting none of those that directly minister to interest; the degree of that directness remaining meanwhile a matter of highly difficult appreciation, and one on which felicity of form and composition . . . mercilessly rests. . . . Really, universally, relations stop nowhere. . . ."

—HENRY JAMES

Connections

Austin Warren

Ann Arbor
The University of Michigan Press

Emily Dickinson's poems reprinted by permission of the publishers and
the Trustees of Amherst College from Thomas H. Johnson, Editor, *The
Poems of Emily Dickinson*, Cambridge, Mass.: The Belknap Press of
Harvard University Press, Copyright, 1951, 1955, by The President and
Fellows of Harvard College.
"If your nerve, deny you . . ." reprinted by permission of Little, Brown
and Company from *The Complete Poems of Emily Dickinson* edited by
Thomas H. Johnson. Copyright 1935 by Martha Dickinson Bianchi;
© 1963 by Mary L. Hampson.

In
Grateful Memory
of
Etta Willis Anderson

Preface

In assembling such a book of essays as this, one is, whatever polite incitations come from without, primarily motivated by the desire to learn for oneself what continuity and coherence unite pieces written over a period of time under differing circumstances and for different occasions and contexts. Some pieces obviously don't belong, are not pieces of a whole. But what common properties are shared by those which remain?

The attempt to choose a title is a useful way of pursuing such an inquiry—even though titles for collections of critical essays, like those for collections of poems, can scarcely avoid being affected, either affectedly fine or affectedly and perhaps arrogantly simple, and though there are fashions in titles as well as in all else. *Rage for Order*, the predecessor of the present book, had, like many such assemblages, a choice phrase from a poem (Wallace Stevens' "Idea of Order") as its title— one adequately representative of the concern with the hierarchic principle which Kenneth Burke found to characterize the book.

Connections, the title chosen for the book I now preface, is a title in another style—one more common in France than with us (having its analogues in *Messages*, *Approximations*, and *Prétextes*). Because E. M. Forster's "only connect" literally furnishes the phrase, I have displayed it as an epigraph, but I really had in mind something less total than the contextual meaning of the phrase as it appears in *Howard's End:* I was thinking, rather more literally, of what Henry James generally called 'relations'—of no single passage in James's critical commentaries but his pervasive emphasis on attaching each particularity to as many other particularities as, by reasonable framing, is possible—the pervasive concern with 'interness.'

What are the connections between the essays here assembled? My first perception, not at all rejected, was that, like the rest of my books, they concern literature in relation to religion and learning (not the 'learning process' and not 'scholarship' but erudite knowledge of the past), and they assume (a highhanded assumption) that the three are capable of operating in collaboration. I do not attempt theoretically to deal with 'literature and religion' or 'literature and erudition,' both topics of philosophic, historical, and practical importance, but to exhibit some cases of coincidence or coinherence. Without denying the virtues of primitive art and the special values produced by autodidacticism (adequately urged in our own time), I cherish, and celebrate, the values and the virtues of 'Culture' and 'Tradition.'

The 'connections' I found between the essays were also those lower on the scale of abstraction. The key to the book is probably the essay on the *Magnalia,* in which Mather is approached through Whittier, Mrs. Stowe, and Hawthorne, writers who read him—a mode of treatment extended, in the note on the essay, to William Carlos Williams. The pattern is not one of 'sources and influences,' nor yet of the 'shock of recognition' (to quote the title of Edmund Wilson's richly suggestive anthology of authors on authors), but, more nearly, the desire to exhibit 'Literature as an Institution' (the phrase, though not the sense, from Harry Levin). Sometimes there are friendships connecting my authors (Benson's with Montague James; More's with Eliot); sometimes the connection is stylistic (three of my prose writers are, by my reckoning, Baroque). Authors who are the center of one essay often occur incidentally or episodically in another. And there are figures without an essay whose appearance is frequent enough to make them count for coherence: Henry James, for example, and Cardinal Newman.

This book is a selection from the essays I have written and (with one exception, that on Montague James) previously published during my twenty years' professorship of literature at The University of Michigan (1948–68).

As a literary critic, I have no 'method,' no specialty, but am what is called, in another discipline, a 'general practitioner.' Literary theory and methodology have ever interested me; but, confronted with the situation of 'practical criticism,' I look through my repertory for the methods and the mixture of methods appropriate to the case before me—in consequence of which the proportion of stylistic analysis to biographical, or biographical to ideological, will be found to vary from essay to essay.

Lastly, some acknowledgments. With one exception these essays originally appeared in literary quarterly reviews—the *Kenyon,* the *Sewanee,* and the *Southern;* and I thank the editors of these reviews for permission to reprint. All the essays, however, have been revised, and some of them completely recast and rewritten, for their publication here. As I have revised the essays, I have become increasingly aware of debts over a long period of time to my late friend, Howard Blake, poet and intellectually exciting talker, and another friend, René Wellek, a man of extraordinary erudition, whose philosophic mind and general sanity and balance quite equal his scholarship.

In preparing the present book, I have had steady and much valued help from Elizabeth Case, till recently executive editor of the University of Michigan Press, and from John Conron, my former assistant and continuing friend. Cheryl Conron has, with considerable patience, typed repeated drafts of the essays; and my wife has been a painstaking corrector of typescripts and proofs and the constant support of the often disheartened reviser.

The Guggenheim Foundation has my thanks for an as yet unacknowledged year of leisure for study, meditation, and writing; and, for a grant providing me with secretarial and

Preface

other clerical assistance in the preparation of this book, I am grateful to the Horace H. Rackham School of Graduate Studies of The University of Michigan.

For friendly offices of sundry and special sorts I am grateful to my friends Leon Edel, Andrew Lytle, Sherman Paul, Donald Stanford, Paul Stanwood, and Tony Stoneburner.

Ann Arbor, August 1969

ACKNOWLEDGMENTS

The essays on Donne and Browne were originally published in the *Kenyon Review;* those on Mather, Emily Dickinson, A. C. Benson, and T. S. Eliot in the *Sewanee Review;* and those on Hawthorne and P. E. More in the *Southern Review;* permission to reprint has been given by the editors of these quarterlies.

Dates of the original appearance are given at the end of each essay.

Contents

The Very Reverend Dr. John Donne

In a letter of 1619, accompanying the manuscript of *Biathanatos*, the writer distinguishes between "Jack Donne," the poet and man about town, and "Dr. Donne," the Anglican priest and preacher. This dichotomy of himself is, clearly, an exaggeration such a man appears forced to make by his own feeling of 'before' and 'after' and the break between them.

Quite clearly, Walton's interpretations are, as theologians say of other theologians' work, "to be read with caution." For one thing, Walton was writing lives of the Anglican saints. For another, his work, first entitled, *The Life and Death of Dr. Donne*, giving predominant space to the 'holy dying,' sought, in parallel to St. Augustine's career and confessions, to tell the tale of a saint who was once a sinner. It is hardly to be doubted that this view of the matter was given its direction by Donne himself: Walton's life may indeed be read as what the aging Donne, Walton's pastor and friend, virtually dictated—both the 'facts' and the attitude.

Attempts to schematize Donne's life remain unconvincing. As a young man, he was never, demonstrably, a rake; nor did he become, in age, a 'saint.' Among his 'juvenilia,' his *Paradoxes and Problems*, is a shrewd little essay called, "Why Do Young Laymen So Much Study Divinity"; and he himself, though not ordained till 1615, when he was in his forties, was, from 1602 on, much engaged in theological and ecclesiastical studies: indeed, in view of his family connections and his intellectual type, it is difficult to suppose a time when he was not.

Of course there is a vast difference between 'study-religion' and the life of a practicing Christian, as Donne was certainly aware; but there is also a very considerable difference between a conscientious clergyman and a saint. After becoming an Anglican priest, Donne appears to have lived an ascetic life, and he did not—though, contrary to the Whistonian heresy held by the Vicar of Wakefield, his church allowed it—remarry. Yet he did not relinquish the desire to marry off his daughters after the fashion which the world calls well, and he held St. Dunstan's benefice in addition to his deanery—a pluralism which a letter shows his felt need to defend. If he should not be grouped with Dean Swift or the Reverend Laurence Sterne, he does not belong with Hooker, Andrewes, Herbert, Ken, and Keble among the Anglican saints.

Not even Walton seems to know when Donne ceased to be a Catholic and became an Anglican. All one can say with moderate assurance is that till after he left the University he remained, in deference to his mother's control, a nominal recusant, and that by the time of his marriage, performed by a priest of the English Church, he must have become, at least ostensibly, an Anglican. There may well have intervened a period when he practiced neither religion—when he was a Pyrrhonist.

Donne's final acceptance of Anglican orders, at the instigation of King James, was made after long delay—delay for which a variety of good reasons may be given: the hope that secular preferment might still be his, consciousness of moral unworthiness, doubts concerning the religion he was called upon to defend.

The intellectual position he finally adopted was not that of an Anglo-Catholic like Andrewes and Laud nor even that of a more 'central' Anglican like George Herbert. He was an Anglican individualist, like F. D. Maurice and W. R. Inge and Phillips Brooks.

He accepted something like the principle of national churches, the principle *cuius regio, eius religio*—maintaining that the Reformed churches had preserved the Christian fundamentals in Scripture, creeds, and sacraments, and holding that order, ecclesiastical as well as political, was preferable to 'scrupulosity.' He did not submit to Canterbury as, in rivalry to Rome, the *one true church;* nor does he press apostolic succession or even the necessity of the episcopate. He allows validity to Lutheran and Calvinist ecclesiasticisms—indeed he comes dangerously near to maintaining that the true Christian Church has existed only *since* the Reformation—though the more cautious implication inferable from the sermons would be that the early Church Fathers had been true Christians but that true Christianity had thereafter lapsed till the advent of Luther.

Donne writes always as a 'Reformed' Christian, for whom Luther and Calvin—more particularly the latter—are authorities to cite. To be sure, he cites also pre-Reformation Fathers of the Western Church and occasionally Doctors, like "our Holkot" —the fourteenth-century English and Oxford Dominican, Robert of Holkot; and from the Eastern Church he cites SS. Athanasius, Basil, Cyril, Gregory. But his proportion and emphasis and tone are different from those of Hooker, Andrewes, and Taylor. Despite his theoretical tolerance, he is less ecumenical, more polemic. Hooker and Andrewes, Montagu and Cosin are Anglicans devoted to their national church not primarily as "by law established" but as an 'idea' of the Catholic Church drawn from the three creeds, the first four Councils, the first five centuries, and as a living spiritual organism continuous from pre-Reformation England, the *Ecclesia Anglicana* of Bede and St. Anselm. Donne, however, has passed from Rome, through skepticism, to a Christianity partly pragmatic, partly personal—which is Anglican negatively or politically rather than positively.

Of course, as an Anglican preacher he attacked both Papists and Puritans; but he is far more voluble and more violent against Rome and especially against the Jesuits, the order dominant in the Counter Reformation and to which, as head of the English Mission, his uncle, Father Jasper Heywood, belonged.

Donne's violence against Rome, sometimes attributed to

his desire to please King James, is surely too constant to be attributed to a single motive. The grounds of his attack are many. Certainly, he regards Papists as loyal to a foreign power and hence as incapable of being loyal Englishmen. But he also attacks Papist greed for money, feigned miracles, additions to the Faith, including Mariolatric developments, the false interpretation and even editing of Scripture and the Fathers. Nor should we forget the possibility of purely personal motives, silent though he remains about them.

Donne's favorite doctors and saints are those who, like himself, were once rhetoricians and philosophers and then, after long struggle, were converted—thereafter dedicating to their new faith their natural and trained talents. Closest to him are St. Paul of Tarsus and St. Augustine of Hippo. His four sermons on the Conversion of St. Paul are of his best. That Donne admired the Epistles we know: "Wheresoever I open St. Paul's Epistles, I meet not words but thunder, and universal thunder, thunder that passes through all the world."

Donne was a close student of the Bible, in Latin and English at least. But Dr. Jessop, who mistakenly calls him a High Churchman, is also mistaken in supposing his insistence on plenary inspiration a sign thereof; for, in the seventeenth century, Anglicans, whether Laudian or Puritan, and Protestants, whether Presbyterian or Brownist, shared with Roman Catholics this conception of Scripture. More of a point might be made of Donne's frequent use of texts from the Old Testament —yet that would, save for the Psalms, suggest rather some inclination toward Puritanism, since the Anglo-Catholics of his century preached chiefly from the Gospels and Epistles, often from those appointed in the liturgy for a specific Sunday or other holy day.

That the 'close reading' of the Bible interested Donne is clear. He is always engaged by problems of methodology and exegesis—how to read a book, a page, a verse, a word. Preaching on "Blessed are the pure in heart," he gives six pages to raising questions about the Sermon on the Mount: Are the discourses in Matthew and Luke one and the same or not? And was each a single discourse or a cento of utterances? And was

John Donne

the sermon a *conscio ad clerum* or *ad populum*, addressed to initiates or all? *Both and*, he answers: We "must preach in the mountain and preach in the plain too." His general rule of exegesis, to which (needless to say) he does not always adhere, is perfectly sound. "Take the words invested in their circumstance, in the context and coherence," and on the same page he illustrates this contextual exegesis by appealing, as he is impressively able to do, to the "collation of places. . . ."

One of his great somber sermons, delivered at Whitehall in 1619, with the text "Woe unto you that desire the day of the Lord . . . ; the day of the Lord is darkness and not light" collates by *differentiae*: This "is not Ezekiel's *Vae pastoribus insipientibus*, which cannot feed their flock, nor Jeremy's *Vae pastoribus disperdentibus*, Woe to those lazy shepherds which do not feed their flock but allow them to scatter"—nor is it the woe pronounced on the "sin of presumption" or the "sin of hypocrisy." Donne takes us down to the woe of "the deepest sin, the sin of desperation"—that deadly sin in which men "grow to a murmuring weariness of this life . . . ," and to the woe of hypocrites in that day "when records of all thoughts shall be laid open," and the woe of those who seek death—either by Stoic suicide or the Jesuit's hunger of "an imagined martyrdom" (the last phrase, from the preface to *Biathanatos*).

As a literary man—nay, an author—Donne can scarcely avoid attending to the 'Bible as literature'; and his literary comments are always engaging.

He distinguishes the *genres* of the Bible. Having remarked that the Psalms are his favorite book in the Old Testament, and St. Paul's Epistles in the New, he explains that both are genres according to literary theory. "St. Paul writes letters; David, poems." A psalm is "such a form as is both curious and requires diligence in the making; and then, when it is made, can have nothing, no syllable, taken from it nor added to it. . . ." "*Job*," he remarks, is a "tragicomedy," the Canticle, "an epithalamion"; the tenth chapter of St. John's Gospel, a "pastoral" ("I am the good shepherd").

In referring to the Scriptures, Donne is careful to distinguish their common author, the Holy Ghost, from the inspired penman of a given portion, sometimes at once distinguishing and coupling the two in such a phrase as "the Holy Ghost, in David. . . ." He comments on the literary styles of the writers—their recurrent metaphors and phrases. The "secretaries of the Holy Ghost . . . do for the most part retain and express in their writings some . . . air of their former professions . . . ; ever inserting into their writings some phrases, some metaphors, some allusions, taken from that profession": "Thus Amos writes as a former shepherd, and Solomon as a former lover of women."

As for recurrent phrases, Moses reiterates "As the Lord liveth, and as I live, saith the Lord," and Jesus, "Verily, verily, I say unto you"; but there are also recurrences not limited to a single inspired penman. Donne preached a Christmas sermon in 1628 on a text—"Lord, who had believed our report"—occurring, as he remarked, in Isaiah, in St. John, and in St. Paul—an idiom of the Holy Ghost's.

In the Third Book of his *Confessions*, St. Augustine confesses his early dissatisfaction with the literary quality of the Scriptures, which seemed to him "unworthy to be compared to the stateliness of Tully"; and St. Jerome is well known to have had his struggle with the rhetorical ghost of Cicero.

Without making any similar confession, Dr. Donne is ever eager to defend the Bible as literarily great. Of "all rhetorical and poetical figures that fall into any art, we are able to produce higher strains, and livelier examples, out of the Scriptures, than out of all the orators or poets in the world. . . ." There are, to be sure, books and passages in which God speaks to the plain and simple man in that man's own language; but "men of larger capacity and more curiosity may hear God in that music that they love best—in a curious, in an harmonious, style unparalleled by any."

In his *Devotions* (Expostulation 19) Donne prays, God, "thou art a figurative, a metaphorical, God. . . . A God in whose words there is such a height of figures, such voyages, such peregrinations to fetch such remote and precious metaphors, such extensions, such spreadings, such curtains of allegories, such Third Heavens of hyperboles, so harmonious elocutions, so retired and so reserved expressions . . . as all profane authors seem of the seed of the serpent that creeps. . . ." This eloquent description of God's literary style sounds strangely like a description of Donne's own: it may at least be said to speak of that part of God as man of letters in whose image and likeness Donne the preacher—yet more than Donne the poet—was made.

The transition between God's style and Donne's is made by that of the great Eastern and Western Fathers of the Church—the great ex-rhetoricians such as SS. Augustine, Basil, and Chrysostom, all favorites with Donne—and such a medieval preacher as St. Bernard. In at least one passage, Donne indeed slips instinctively from the Bible to the Patristic preachers. "The Holy Ghost is figurative; and the Fathers are wanton in their spiritual elegancies, such as that of St. Augustine's . . . and such other harmonious, and melodious, and mellifluous cadences of these waters of life."

Donne follows the Fathers in despoiling the Egyptians of their jewels; and from his sermons, as from the writings of St. Augustine and St. Francis of Sales, one might illustrate all the schemes and tropes of Quintilian's *Institutes*. Especially prominent is the figure *homoeoteleuton*, the classical prose approximation to rhyme—often one should say to semantic rhyme, since the phonetic consonance but stresses a parallelism or antithesis of conception: as it does when Donne cites St. Bernard as, in "his musical and harmonious cadences," saying, "*Pax non promissa, sed missa* . . . not promised, but already sent; *non dilata, sed data*, not treated, but concluded; *non prophetata, sed praesentata* . . .*"; or when Donne himself says, "Only in heaven shall God proceed to this patefaction, this manifestation, this revelation of himself. . . ."

As he delights in similarities of cadence, so in those of initiation, remarking "How much, and how often, St. Paul delights himself in that *sociable* syllable *syn, con: conregnare* and *convivificare*, and *consedere*"; and he likes the Patristic and Baroque *chiasmus:* in an Easter sermon, he speaks of the per-

7

sons at the tomb as "angelical women and evangelical angels."

The specimens quoted, for another purpose, should make evident one marked character of Donne's pulpit style. Like the other great masters of Jacobean and Caroline prose, whether Burton or Browne, Andrewes or Taylor, he wrote for an audience which knew Latin: he was himself at least as familiar with St. Jerome's Vulgate as with English versions of the Scriptures. Donne's Latinity, whether quotation or Anglicization, is not to be regretted. The amplitude and magnificence of the great sermons require and justify the coupling, matched only by Browne's, of learned diction and plain. And, as with Burton and Browne, Donne rarely leaves his direct quotations isolated. They give him the rhetorical occasion for gloss, free paraphrase, expansion, development. Thus, in a sermon on St. Paul's conversion, he remarks, "It was a wise and pious counsel that Gamaliel gave. . . . *Abstinet:* Forbear a while; *give God sea-room;* give Him His latitude; and you may find that you mistook at first. . . ."

Most of all, this great Jacobean style bears witness, as, linguistically, we can no longer do—as not even Joyce could do—to English literature as at once regional, 'national,' and European.

Donne was not an original or a systematic theologian; but he was a great preacher: I venture to think a greater preacher than poet—able to express in that medium, and in that middle period of life, a range and depth to which the poems rarely reach. In the introduction to his 1919 selection from Donne's sermons, Logan Pearsall Smith rightly remarks that the sermon is a form of literary expression which—"since its subject matter is nothing less than the whole of life"—"gives the widest possible scope to a great preacher," and, again, that the dealing with good and evil, the brevity of life and the mystery of death, "is the mood of religion in whatever Dogmas it may be clothed."

As seventeenth-century writers are fond of quoting, "The blessed Magdalen changed not her passion but its object." In changing from poet to preacher, Donne was not unclothed but clothed upon (2 Cor. 5:4). He remained the same astute and piercing self-analyst and analyst of others he had ever been. Of English preacher-psychologists, only Newman is his equal. He says—and often, certainly, out of self-knowledge—the things which must have made each who heard him wonder, How knows this man my own special sin? Here are a few examples. Coming to divine service is not enough: the motives must be right. Many a man "hears but the logic, or the rhetoric, or the ethic, or the poetry, of the sermon; but the *sermon of the sermon* he hears not."

"The mind of a curious man delights," with the *libido sciendi,* "to examine itself upon interrogatories which, upon the rack, it cannot answer, and to vex itself with such doubts as it cannot resolve. . . ."

The scrupulous man "shall suspect his religion, suspect his repentance, suspect the comforts [absolution] of the minister, suspect the efficacy of the Sacrament, suspect the mercy of God Himself."

A man may not literally have committed adultery; yet "he may have done that in a *look,* in a *letter,* in a *word,* in a *wish* . . ."; so "that man is a murderer that stabs as deep as he can, though it be with his tongue, with his pen, with his frown."

As a preacher, Donne, whose extant sermons number a hundred and sixty, is uneven. Sometimes he is wearisomely pedantic, sometimes a show-off; sometimes eccentric: of his three marriage sermons, none happy efforts, the most ambitious is preached from the perversely inapposite text, "In Heaven there is no marrying or giving in marriage." But he is sometimes coherent and magnificent throughout—notably in his sermons on the second and fourth verses of Psalm 38.

In 1928, the then recent convert to Anglicanism, T. S. Eliot used Dean Donne as a foil to his celebration of Bishop Lancelot Andrewes: the contrasts between the sermons of the two is effectively made. Donne's sermons, he points out, abound in striking passages of rhetoric and psychological analysis but correspondingly lack the continuity and structural integrality of Andrewes'; and Andrewes' sermons are meditations on God and the objective realities of the spiritual world, while Donne's, more "modern," characteristically show more interest in man's side of the religious transaction, explore the labyrinth of the human heart, its evasions and recalcitrances. "In his thought, Donne has . . . much more in common with [his educators] Jesuits, and, on the other hand, much more in common with the Calvinists" than has Andrewes—whose religion, essentially medieval, and so based on dogma, prayer, and liturgy, antedates both Reformation and Counter Reformation.

Eliot charges that Donne, by comparison with Andrewes, was an impure preacher, because, partly at least, he used the sermon as a form of self-expression. Donne had, it is admitted, a genuine taste for theology and he had "religious emotion"; but he lacked any native aptitude for the spiritual life. His tumultuous nature found refuge and bulwark in religion; what he found, however, was a substitute for other activities and values, not a totally other thing, a totally new life. He was, in sum, a "personality in the romantic sense of the word."

Offered with Eliot's characteristic qualifications and hesitancies, the contentions of his essay can be accepted—perhaps, though it scarcely seems that only men with a congenital spirituality should be qualified to preach to fallen women and men; for a fellow sinner, saved by grace or the sacraments, might seem better able to speak to their condition. But one knows what Eliot means, and says with some inexactness; one's own feelings about Donne as a preacher are mixed. Personality in the Christian or the classical sense is requisite in a preacher. As against the collective and communal voice of the liturgy, we desire to hear from the preacher an individual voice, personally affirming in his own idiom the collective wisdom of the liturgy. But this necessary degree of selfhood Donne does appear to have overpassed. When we praise the coherence and magnificence of the grandiose final sermon, "Death's Duel," we have some regret that it was the prospect of the preacher's own very imminent death which brought him to such heights.

1954

The Styles of Sir Thomas Browne

We should distinguish between *Style* and *a style*. Speaking normatively and evaluatively, we praise the presence of Style; speaking descriptively, we hold that every author has a style, and turn our attention to analyzing its specific character in this author or that. Yet the two concepts are not completely alternative; for, if all authors have a style, some of them—a minority—participate in Style.

Browne is one of those thus doubly endowed. He both has a style, a markedly characteristic one, and he merits, according to almost universal consent for at least a century and a half, high position among English writers who have Style.

Those who are said to have Style—whom hereafter we may call 'stylists'—have, at least up till now, always been representatives of the 'grand style' (Johnson, Burke, and Gibbon) or of poetic prose (De Quincey and Ruskin), or writers like Jeremy Taylor, Newman, and the later Henry James, who, though perhaps inexactly called either 'grand' or 'poetic,' yet have an elegance and opulence in excess of purely expressive needs. All of these, it would appear, belong to the tradition devoted to the phonetic figures called by the ancients *schemes*, to euphony and cadence—to ornament, to what the Renaissance called *copia* (richness, not in the sense of compactness but in the sense of inexhaustible abundance), to development not by selection but by expansion. Masters of the 'plain style,' like Swift, Cobbett, and Franklin, have never, it seems, been given the honorific title of *stylist*—nor, commonly, have such masters of the 'middle style' as Addison and Jane Austen.

This restriction suggests the concept of style which Croce, with much justification, rejected as one of applied ornament and which certainly suffers from the rigidity of its caste distinctions. We should, I think, abandon such use of the term 'style', unrestricted by generic epithets like *grand* or *poetic*, as inacceptably normative.

Style is not something external to 'meaning'—even when the style is 'grand.' Rhetoric need not be 'mere' rhetoric. And it is patently old-fashioned and 'pseudo-classical' to identify style with the 'grand style.' But I think it possible to conceive and name modernly the shared character of the famous Stylists. They are those authors whose linguistic form is most expressive, most closely integrated; whose writing seems most spiritually signed and identifiable. Their distinction as writers is closely bound up with their vocabulary and syntax and rhythm; the 'meaning' of their works is, like the 'meaning' of poems, correspondingly difficult to translate or to summarize. Style, as W. K. Wimsatt finely defines it, is "the last and most detailed elaboration of meaning." Though this definition is applicable to any author, the 'stylist' is he who, at this stage or level, achieves his distinction: whose originality lies not in his big ideas (his major concepts, often philosophically derivative and 'eclectic') but in his discriminations and nuances, in his intellectual sensibility.

In speaking thus much of Style, I have said much which is relevant to style: the difference between the two may be ultimately quantitative—the degree of expressiveness.

Modern stylistics is a brave effort to produce an objective literary analysis. It defines style as the "expressive system of a work, of an author, or of a period," and then seeks to infer or induce from the linguistic traits of an author the spiritual (the psychological or philosophical) character which they 'express' —as some critics have sought to reconstruct the Baroque *Geist* from its tropes of catachresis, oxymoron, and paradox.

But has a writer only one style? Shall we not speak rather of the *styles* of Shakespeare, or even of Milton? It would be easier to characterize, clearly and sharply, the style of *Love's*

Labour's Lost and the style of *The Tempest* than to characterize Shakespeare's style; yet it would seem to be an article of
faith in the metaphysics of literature that there must be a perceptible and describable integrity to the life work of a great
writer, perceptible in the continuity and development of his
style.

A writer develops, or at any rate, changes, from style to
style. His style may mature, then decay—perhaps into an exaggeration or even parody of itself.

Again, a writer may adjust his style to his audience, his
theme, his occasion—in short, to the proprieties of his genre.
There is the aesthetic principle of decorum, or *keeping*.

Classical antiquity and the Renaissance postulate a hierarchy of styles. Thus 'grand' style is for persons of grandeur
to use for grand purposes on grand occasions; otherwise it becomes absurd, pathetic, or disgusting, becomes bombast and ir-
relevance.

There are, to be sure, persons who, on grounds of con-
venience, inflexibility, or principle adopt an invariable garb
—the clerical black of the priest, the leather suit of George
Fox, the sober and plain habit of Shakers and Mennonites, the
archaic mode retained by a gentleman of the 'last age,' or the
anticipation of some future mode. The uniform is a witness to
a simple conception of integrity: it is keeping one's hat on in
the presence of kings, or one's crown on while traveling in the
subway or visiting the zoo.

Natural, if finally inadequate, is the analogy of style and
dress. Some writers appear to have but one style, used upon all
occasions; the later Johnson and the later Henry James are
judged to be such. Johnson was accused of 'talking *Ramblers*';
the anecdotes of James report his directions to chauffeurs and
addresses to children as never less than ripely James. In such
cases a man devises or creates a style suited to express and sustain his characteristic or dominant attitude and interests, but
then the style, like the institution a man has founded, acquires
an existence of its own, and, at last, may make a man say what
it intends, the tune prescribing the words.

Johnson and James were awkward and embarrassed in the world of things and gadgets; their masterly ease was taken in a verbalized world of qualities and relations. Both were capable of parodying their own styles, and the parody is a kind of ironic recognition that the language capable of serving a man's needs in his own country cannot be expected to serve *in partibus infidelium*.

Curiously, and indeed bafflingly, Browne, who might seem to belong with Johnson and James, with Coleridge and Father Hopkins, does not. Dr. Browne's letters addressed to his sons, and concerned with facts and practical life, are composed in a style scarcely recognizable as that of the ornate Sir Thomas. He writes to his son Edward, physician in London:

> Pray present my service to Sir John Hinton when you see him; 'tis a long time ago since I had the honor to know him beyond sea. Mr. Norton married Sir Edmund Bacon's daughter, who was a very good lady and died last summer, and I think he was a member of the last parliament. Perform your business with the best ease you can, yet giving everyone sufficient content. I believe my Lady O'Bryon is by this time in better health and safety; though hypochondriac and splenetic persons are not long from complaining, yet they may be good patients, and may be borne withall, especially if they be good-natured.

A cherisher of Browne's literary mysticism may well be disturbed upon first discovering his letters. Browne ought, it seems, to have been incapable of such discourse. Then, recalling the familiar paradox of the mystics, that they are often practical and even successful organizers and administrators, one feels, at least temporarily, reassured that his integrity may yet be inviolate.

It is at any event clear that Browne is not the writer of a single style, rich but rigid. Though our persistent idea of Browne is likely to be of a compulsive writer, not readily conscious of what he is moved to do, we must revise it to that of a writer knowing of modes and textures. In an essay on Browne,

Sir Thomas Browne

John Addington Symonds shrewdly suggests, "There is a sustained paradox in his thought which does not seem to belong to the man so much as to the artist." Impressive critical analyses have been made on the basis of a single work. Croll's examples, in "The Baroque Style," are all drawn from the *Religio;* Saintsbury's study of Browne's prose rhythm is restricted to the fifth chapter of *Hydriotaphia.* Hostile criticism has often taken as typical the style of *Christian Morals,* written at the end of his life and unpublished till 1756—a work showing signs of decadence in its exaggeration and stiffening of Brunonian traits. In diction it is the most insistently Latinic; in sentence structure the most Senecan and aphoristic. The wit has lost resourcefulness and gaiety; its devices have become—what they were not in Browne's earlier work—predictable.

Browne has at least three styles—a low, a middle, and a high—the low represented by *Vulgar Errors,* the high by the *Garden of Cyrus,* the medium by *Religio* and (in decadent form) by *Christian Morals.*

The basis for differentiation is primarily one of generic decorum. Without doubt, Browne designed *Vulgar Errors* as a contribution to "philosophy" and the advancement of learning, a fulfillment of one of Bacon's proposals, not as a piece of literature. He composed with his Commonplace Books before him, attempting to transfer his notes into his folio after the manner of an academic dissertation, and to write a sober, straightforward, technical style.

The *Religio* is his masterpiece in the middle style. In a brilliant essay on "Seventeenth Century Prose," Francis Thompson called attention to the Silver Latin antecedent of the *stile coupé.* In contrast to the "Ciceronian Hooker," Browne is found "steeped in classic models more compact and pregnant than Cicero. Like his French contemporaries, he was influenced by the great Latin rhetoricians—Lucan, and Seneca, whose rivalry it was to put an idea into the fewest possible words." Thompson is most struck by Browne's "serried" style (the *stile coupé*). Yet at least as frequent in the *Religio* is the "loose or libertine style," associated with Pyrrhonism and Montaigne, which expresses the movement of ordering the mind in the process of thinking. Syntactically, this is a style in which the sentences, beginning with the main clause, proceed by annexation and juxtaposition of relative and adverbial clauses, participial or prepositional phrases—rhetoric and logic triumphing over grammar. The serried style and the loose style, in sensitive intermixture and proportion, compose Browne's middle manner.

Urn Burial and the *Garden of Cyrus*, both written in Browne's fifties and published as a single volume, share a generic character, even though we have no term for it. They are artistic compositions, prose poems, meditations. *Religio* is an intellectual autobiography, a 'familiar essay'; *Vulgar Errors*, by its author's intention, is a work of instruction and enlightenment, soberly expository. But the two prose poems, though they may at first appear to be on or about topics, are but speciously so. As one needs no experience of fishing to follow, with delight, Walton's *Angler,* so one need have no extrinsic interest in Browne's scholarly materials. Out of facts, antiquarian or scientific, he makes poetico-philosophical meditations.

It is these two essays which raise the question of prose rhythm. Some theorists exclude the study of rhythm from stylistics on the assumption that stylistics deals with the expressive, and that rhythm, whether in verse or prose, is rhetorical or decorative—not integral to the meaning of a literary work. In my judgment, however, prose rhythm belongs to stylistics; has expressive as well as formal character. It has a formal character generically expressive.

In terms of the two rival traditions of prose style, the Ciceronian (or oratorical) and the Senecan (or philosophical), the tropes or thought-figures, like metaphor and paradox, belong to the latter; the schemes, or sound figures, under which the *cursus*—like rhyme and alliteration—was classified, belong to the oratorical, or ornate, tradition.

The distinguished historian of style, Morris Croll, who divided prose masters into the orators and the essayists, named Browne as (along with Seneca, the presumed master of essayists), "fond of the cadences of oratory." The collects of the Anglican Prayer Book, so familiar to Browne, offer identifiable versions of the Latin *cursus* or cadence; and there are easily audible specimens of the *cursus* in Browne. The first pattern of the *planus*, a dactyl followed by a trochee, gives, in Latin, *potentiam suam;* in the Prayer Book, "help and defend us"; in Browne, "Christian religion," "noble believers." The frequent use of the *Tardus*, ending with a trisyllable, contributes much to the Latinate grandiosity of Browne and Gibbon; from *Urn Burial* come these cadences: "There were a happiness," "life of Methusaleh," "our last necessity," "princes and counselors," "restless inquietude." Still more impressive is the second pattern of *Tardus*, with its stresses on the third and seventh syllables, counted from the end of the cadence: "antiquates antiquities," "balsam of our memories," "angles of contingency," "raptures of futurity."

Cadences are frequent and a marked feature of style in *Hydriotaphia*, comparatively rare in *Religio*, and almost absent from *Vulgar Errors*. That is to say: they are inappropriate to expository writing, but, as Browne's discourse becomes more general and more poetic, as it becomes *oraison funèbre*, it becomes also cadential. Surely, then, there is an expressive character to the use of the phonetic device. It marks, and partly makes, the shift of tone.

Browne's celebrated diction is as calculated as the other features of his writing. Corroboratory evidence is his short, ninth tract, "Of Language," which includes six specimens of "Saxon," composed by Browne, to show what pre-Conquest English, or West Saxon, was like, together with word for word paraphrases into a modern English admitting no word of Latin or Romance origin.

His specimen of modern English keeping to "Saxon" roots does not exaggerate the contrast between English monosyllables and polysyllabic Latin, but offers "unworthy," "almighty," "manifold," "unrighteousness," and copious disyllables. And he characterizes English as a language Saxon in its system of relationships, or syntax, into which substantives and modifiers of other origin can readily be fitted. These observations are consistent with what has been generally observed—that though Browne's diction is Latin his sentence structure, unlike Milton's, rarely is.

Why did Browne not write in Latin? The question is engaging; the answer not obvious. In the preface to *Vulgar Errors* he rules out any notion that his choice was motivated by the desire to dispel those errors from the "vulgar"—from readers limited to the vernacular. He avowedly addressed those English gentlemen whose modern equivalents retain enough of their college Latin to profit, in some degree, from the left-hand page of the Loeb Library: his first readers must have known some Latin to understand his English, for the technicality of the subject, as he says in the same preface, "will sometimes carry us into expressions beyond mere English apprehensions. And indeed, if elegancy still proceedeth, and English pens maintain that stream we have of late observed to flow from many, we shall within few years be fain to learn Latin to understand English, and a work will prove of equal facility in either." He raises the fancy of a literary Esperanto equidistant from English and Latin.

To such a general amphibian as Browne, one can plausibly attribute the preference of a 'macaroni' language over a straight, and a personally compounded over an inherited. One might suppose the scientist responsible for the Anglo-Saxonism, and the mystic and artist for the Latinic; but the hypothesis does not work: both the scientist and the Christian Platonist, or Gnostic, in Browne, are linguistically on the same side. His one violence of attitude, his one antipathy, is against the masses —whom he commonly calls the "vulgar"; and the errors against which he inveighs are allegedly "vulgar errors," not the heresies of intellectuals. Latinity—whether scientific, theological, or literary—is the mark of the intellectual, of the citizen of the world, the 'good European,' and the inheritor of Greco-Roman culture, of Mediterranean civilization. Browne is an intellectual snob: one of the most charming of the kind, indeed, yet a natural Gnostic and initiate of the Hermetic Way. The Anglo-Saxon constituent of his style is more difficult to relate to a corresponding element in his thought and nature. We can say, of course, that Sir Thomas is a loyal Englishman and communicant of the Anglican Church—as well as a Christian Platonist; and we can call attention to his study of Old English and his clear assumption that the syntax and the relational words of English would remain "Saxon" while the substantives and adjectives might, with profit, have large augmentation from the "everlasting languages," as he calls Latin and Greek. Or we can say that the "Saxon" element corresponds to that practical side shown in letters to his son—the matter of fact, common-sense side which was obviously not wanting.

Now, reversing our direction, let us start from attitude and tone, while directing our aim at correlative patterns of syntax and diction. One *persona* of Browne is speculative, casuistical, and skeptical: delights in accumulating *catenae* of intellectual difficulties, baffling questions, scruples, distinctions, and qualifications. This Browne, like the corresponding Newman, expresses itself in long sentences proceeding by annexations and parentheses. There is another Browne who is a Stoic and a pragmatist, aphoristic of utterance: "The heart of man is the place devils dwell in," "The man without a navel yet lives in me." "If thou hast not mercy for others, yet be not cruel unto thyself."

Yet it cannot be neatly concluded that Browne identified the aphoristic with the Saxon. He writes, " 'Tis too late to be ambitious"; "There is nothing strictly immortal but immortality"; and the most relentlessly aphoristic work of Browne's is also the most Latinate, the *Christian Morals:* "Move circumspectly, not meticulously; and rather carefully sollicitous than anxiously sollicitudinous." There is no need that the aphoristic sentence be a saying of the folk.

Browne has a general consciousness of the two linguistic lines he is uniting. In the *Religio,* there is a constant use of doublets, Latin and English, the international word and the regional: "a stair, or manifest scale, of creatures." The Angels are certainly the "magisterial and master-pieces of creation." In these examples, there is a general syllabic and rhythmic equivalence; but in others the Latin correlate gives also a climactic prolongation or cadence: "the fire and scintillation of that noble essence," God; the "warm gale and gentle ventilation of this Spirit," "that name and compellation of 'Little flock.' . . ."

The doublets, here Latin and Saxon, turn, in *Christian Morals*, to the coupling of abstract and concrete: "To well manage our Affections and wild Horses of Plato"—"the Areopagy and dark Tribunal of your hearts."

As metaphorist, Browne has no such originality as Donne, Herbert, or Cleveland. He is almost completely lacking in visual imagery or other overt thrust into the writing of the world unsubdued to language. Of martyrs he wrote, he who was tolerant but not courageous, who was a man of culture, not of passion or action, "They may sit in the orchestra and noblest seats of Heaven, who have held up shaking hands in the fire and humanly contended." But I cannot claim the wonderful epithet, "shaking," as characteristic.

His characteristic figures are, at one extreme, sound patterns, and, at the other, logical or etymological figures. In view of his amphibian nature, oxymoron is unexpectedly rare; his Pascalian "man is a noble animal," a special case. This trope, with its coupling of adjective and noun in opposition, is probably too showy or sensational for Browne. More proper are metaphysical puns, uniting sound with sense: "The last and lasting part"; "Time, which antiquates antiquities"; "To strenuous minds, there is an inquietude in over-quietness, and no laboriousness in labor.

There is an aspect of Browne's diction to consider which is to consider also his total meaning: his use of epistemological terms—words and phrases showing his constant sense of the realms of discourse, the context within which a statement is being made.

There is, first of all, his naming of the great traditional divisions of knowledge—Divinity, Metaphysics, Philosophy (by which, of course, Browne means natural science), Logic, and Rhetoric (under which Poetics is subsumed). Then there is his witty use of technical terms from Grammar, Rhetoric, and Logic. "That Rhetorical sentence and Antimetathesis of Augustine. . . ." In God, there is no distinction of tenses. "Who . . . can speak of Eternity without a solecism?"

The main use of these terms is structural. Though in a world of intellectual unity, the trivium and the quadrivium would be hierarchic but also mutually consistent, there is still a latent tension of claims between these modes of contemplative activity; of this, Browne is steadily aware, though not upset or disturbed by it. "In Philosophy, where truth seems double faced, there is no man more paradoxical than myself; but in Divinity. . . ."

There is the contrast between what the nineteenth century called science and religion; but the persistent opposition in Browne is, rather, between logic and rhetoric. Logic is the discipline of reason; rhetoric, an appeal to the imagination. Many things in the *Religio,* says Browne, are "delivered Rhetorically"; many expressions are "merely Tropical"; and "there are many things to be taken in a soft and flexible sense, and not to be called unto the rigid test of Reason."

More generally, one feels the constant presence in Browne's writing of the grammar, or logic, of belief—the levels or degrees of assent. Here one is again reminded of Newman and such distinctions of his as, "Ten thousand difficulties do not make a single doubt."

A kind of *catena* or litany can be drawn from the *Religio:* "to speak more narrowly," "to speak strictly," "to speak properly"; "I am, I confess, naturally inclined to . . . ;" a heresy "I did never positively maintain . . . but have often wished had been consonant to Truth. . . ." "These opinions I have never maintained with pertinacity. . . ." "If we shall literally understand it. . . ." "If we shall strictly examine. . . ." "I can neither prove nor absolutely deny that. . . ." "I do believe that," "I wonder how," "It is a riddle to me now," "I could easily believe that," "Now if you demand my opinion, I confess. . . ."

And here is another litany of the degrees of assent. The archetypal pattern of this, an eminently characteristic kind of Brunonian sentence, is an indefinite number of noun or adverbial clauses beginning *what* or *whether* and terminated by a brief main clause in the form of a cadence. "But whether the ancient Germans, who burned their dead, held any such fear to pollute their deity of Hertha, or the earth, we have no authentic conjecture. . . ." "Or whether . . . it cannot pass without some question"—"Whether . . . may favorably be doubted," "But whether . . . were a query too sad to insist on."

These extraordinary sentences, in which a catalogue of dubieties terminates in a cadence of melancholy—these "notes and queries" set to music, give the chief basis for the charge against Browne, first made in his lifetime and most effectively—almost convincingly—put by Ziegler's *In Divided and Distinguished Worlds*. If one is to reconstruct the spirit of Browne from these sentences, of one type eminently characteristic of him, one might plausibly conclude that, if not an atheist, he was a skeptic. But taken in conjunction with other characteristic types of sentences—notably the aphorism—I read them as the thought-form of an inquiring, even a speculative, mind which delights to entertain conjectures and to ask unanswerable questions for the sake of the vistas they open.

Encyclopedic in his interests, he is something of a laboratory scientist, something of a skeptic (but after the mode to be hyphenated, as also in Pascal, with *fideist*)—even something of a mystic. A believer in a pluralist epistemology, in the concomitance of three or four modes of knowledge, he was unable —and aware that he was unable—to harmonize them all into an impregnable system; yet he was tranquilly confident of their ultimate concord.

"Or whether . . . it cannot pass without some question" is countered by "Life is a pure flame, and we live by an invisible Sun within us." *The Garden of Cyrus*, almost at the end, still has space for questions, Biblical and biological—"Why Joseph designed five changes of raiment unto Benjamin, and David took just five pebbles out of the brook against the Pagan champion?" and "Why amongst sea-stars nature chiefly delighted in five points?" But we end with resolution, with faith that all these questions have an answer, though we may not know it. "All things began in order; so shall they end, and so shall they begin again, according to the Ordainer of order and mystical mathematics of the City of Heaven."

1951

Dr. Cotton Mather's Magnalia

The old New England poet, Whittier,—the good gray celibate Quaker abolitionist poet,—had no love for Dr. Cotton Mather, that determined foe of all enthusiasms, nor for the Puritans who persecuted the Quaker boy, "The Gentle Boy" of Hawthorne's idyllic tale. But, hostile as he was, Whittier still justly apprehended one of Mather's 'notes'—his insatiable curiosity, whether for things natural, or scholastical, or supernatural.

In his preface to his poem, "The Double-Headed Snake of Newbury" (Mass.), Whittier quotes a letter to Mather written by the Reverend Christopher Toppan (Harvard, 1691), pastor of Newbury's East Church, "Concerning the Amphisbaena, as soon as I received your commands, I made diligent inquiry . . . ," the letter begins; and receipt of it, so the poet imagines, sent Mather "galloping" down to Newbury Town.

> *With his eyes agog and his ears set wide,*
> *And his marvelous inkhorn at his side;*
> *Stirring the while in the shallow pool*
> *Of his brains for the lore he learned at school,*
> *To garnish the story, with here a streak*
> *Of Latin and there another of Greek,*
> *And the tales he heard and the notes he took,*
> *Behold! are they not in his Wonder Book?*

Whittier's last line presumably combines a reference to Mather's *Wonders of the Invisible World*, his 1693 monograph on demonology and witchcraft (in which the amphisbaena— to be found in medieval bestiaries and, naturally, in Sir

Thomas Browne's *Vulgar Errors*—does not occur) with a delicate allusion to Hawthorne's *Wonder Book* (1852) and another
allusion, to Joshua 10:13: "Is not this written in the book of
Jasher?"

The amphisbaena, the serpent with a head at each
end, appears in none of Mather's published books but in a com-
munication to the Royal Society of London. Yet of course it
might have; for where in Mather shall we not be prepared to
encounter wonders?

As for the amphisbaena, it never existed, save in the bestiaries; as for the Book of Jasher, it has disappeared. But Mather's monumental Wonder Book, which Whittier knew and
used, the *Magnalia Christi Americana*, published in folio at
London in 1702, is real and still survives.

It is Mrs. Stowe, the daughter of one eminent Congregational parson and the wife of another, who takes the family
liberty of giving Dr. Mather, that encyclopedic scholar, one of
the most 'familiar' epithets. She calls him "that delightful old
New England grandmother whose nursery tales" of New England's "infancy and childhood may well be pondered by those
who would fully understand its far-reaching maturity." And
then she explains what may sound like condescension: "As . . .
I have high ideas of the wisdom of grandmothers, I do our beloved gossip Dr. Cotton Mather the highest possible compli-
ment in granting him the title"; and the twenty-ninth chapter
of her *Oldtown Folks* goes far to substantiate her frivolously
earnest characterization.

Mrs. Stowe strangely lights up the *Magnalia*, Mather's Big
Book, his almost great book—giving back generously with her
right hand what she appears to take away with her left. The
grandmother with her "nursery tales," the "beloved gossip"—
what contemptuous terms for the most learned man of seventeenth-century New England, the Doctor of Divinity from the
University of Glasgow, the Fellow of the Royal Society! Yet
her phrases convey the notion that the importance of the *Magnalia* lies less in its claims to historical accuracy, its sheer factual veracity (whatever may be the credit to be given this

claim), than in its accumulation of oral tradition, its being the vehicular thesaurus of what Mather and his family, especially Dr. Increase Mather, his father, president of Harvard (as Dr. Cotton wished to be, but never succeeded in being), believed Puritan orthodoxy to mean and to be. That Mather sincerely believed it to be history is itself a matter of history, a fact. Indeed, as a matter of fact, we can never reach a history which is not selected and interpreted: at least, anything else is but chronicle—scholarship arranging its archaeological potsherds.

In any case, surely the traditional wisdom of the 'grandmother' is richer and wiser than the arid knowledge of the maiden aunt. And, if Mather is an unconscious mythologist as well as chronicler, because he believed in stories, so much the better.

The *Magnalia* is a book ever to be read—or read in—with delight. In many ways it is also, as its author designed it, a conscious masterpiece written in the Baroque style—one of the last and latest works anywhere written in such a style, belatedly Baroque, as Mather's view of the world is also dominantly (despite his inoculatory daring and his philanthropies) belatedly Baroque.

I

It labors under some serious handicaps. One is Mather's lack of a sense of humor (a gift necessary less that we should use it than that we should not be unintentionally absurd). In his massive "General Introduction," it is incredible to find him wondering how "the modern critics" of 1700 will judge his book, and thinking that some of them may find his style low—"simple, submiss, and humble"; it is indeed so incredible that the rest of the paragraph has to go to defending himself against the opposite view that it is "embellished with too much ornament." And into the same "Introduction" there must needs enter an account of how difficult finding time to write this book was for a busy man with so many other things to do—the busyness of the pastor of the great church in "Boston, the Metropolis of the English America."

Damage is also done to the book by Mather's New Englandly thrifty desire to "gather up the fragments that nothing be lost" (John 6:12). Our divine, eager to speak and write, was also avid of print. The total number of his published works is variously estimated at somewhere between three and four hundred, even though many of these were sermons or tracts—relatively brief. And the folio *Magnalia*, even if not "chiefly a collection of what the author had before printed on historical and biographical subjects" (the admission of its 1855 editor, Samuel G. Drake), is inclusive of pieces too oversized for proportion and continuity. Three may be cited: "The Life of His Excellency Sir William Phips" (a native Massachusettian of humble origin who became a Royal Governor of the Bay State and a member of Dr. Mather's own North Church), "The Life of the Renowned John Eliot" (the most notable converter of 'praying Indians'), and Mather's eloquent Boston lecture of 1698, "The Bostonian Ebenezer: Some Historical Remarks on the State of Boston, the Chief Town of New-England, and of the English America . . ." from the text, 1 Sam. 7:12, "Then Samuel took a stone and set it up, and called the name of it EBEN EZER, saying, Hitherto the Lord hath helped us." All these pieces have, severally, their justifications. Yet what a pity that our Mather, copious and thrifty, could not have carved and cut and thrown away and disposed to form and order and proportion his memorable stones of remembrance. Even more than when he lovingly accumulates, the Lord is with the artist when, painfully, he discards.

Lastly, damage is done to the book by its sadly anticlimactic Seventh and Last Book, called "Ecclesiarum Proelia, or The Wars of the Lord"—a title so ample and vague that it might be, and is, about almost anything. It is Biblical, of course: all the Wars of the Chosen People—whether against the Amalakites or the Amorites or the Philistines or the Canaanites or the Babylonians or the Assyrians—were Wars of the Lord. The Book contains nothing about 'witchcraft,' but jumbles together with little logic and less art the sufferings of the Holy Commonwealth at the hands of Roger Williams and

Anne Hutchinson, next the Quakers (who first disturbed Boston in 1656 and—though allowed to depart peacefully for Rhode Island, that refuge of heretics, kept returning to Boston to 'bear witness' and obtain, if possible, the martyr's crown), then men falsely pretending to be clergymen, and, lastly, the Indian massacres. These sundry threats and annoyances to Zion are held together, indeed, only by assumption, rarely made overt, that Satan, furious at having his territory, that of the devil-worshipping Indians, taken away from him, and at the prospect of a truly Reformed Church, a model to the rest of the world, even England and Europe, set up in his domain, is responsible for all, and the subsidiary assumption that the sins of New Englanders (their lapse from what, in a sermon preached in 1706, was called "The Good Old Way") are being chastised, even as were those 'whorings after false Gods' so ceaselessly denounced by the authorized prophets of the Chosen People of Old. What between enemies without and enemies within, 'true religion' has always had a hard time of it.

Dr. Mather had no hesitation in lashing out at the enemies within. Roger Williams is compared to a "certain windmill in the Low Countries," which, by its rapid motion, fired first the mill and then set a whole town on fire. "But I can tell my reader that, about twenty years before this, there was a whole country in America like to be set on fire by rapid motion of a windmill in the head of one particular person." Indeed, if steadfastness of opinion be the criterion, Williams (like Orestes Brownson) would seem an unsafe guide today; and his "quixotism," as Mather calls it, his movement from opposing the Church of England to opposing Puritan reading of the New Testament in the dogmatic light of the Old, his denial that the King of England had any right to give land belonging to the Indians to Puritans, his passage from Puritan semiorthodoxy to antipaedobaptism and from that to se-baptism and from that to the vague position of Seeker—all this, together with his tolerant willingness that men of all religions, even Quakers, might live in Providence Plantations, would still damn the author of *The Bloody Tenent of Persecution for Conscience's Sake.*

That he used many endeavors to Christianize the Indians in his neighborhood is commendable; so, too, is the fact that, as an old man, he debated orally against Quakers and published against them; yet these are merits which but mitigate his central offenses against the Puritan Establishment.

Mrs. Hutchinson is more violently treated, doubtless because, though a woman and not eligible for preacherdom, she yet nearly seduced, doctrinally, the great John Cotton, the glory of the New England Church. "*Dux femina facta.*" "It is the mark of seducers that they lead captive silly women; but what will you say when you hear of subtle women becoming the most remarkable of the seducers?" After her antinomian utterances and claims to special divine inspirations, after it was found there was "no hope of reclaiming her from scandalous, dangerous, and enchanting extravagancies," this dame was excommunicated and ordered to depart out of the colony; and, Rhode Island, the "Gerizzim of New England," not proving sanctuary enough for her, she removed to Long Island, where the Indians "treacherously" killed her and her family.

II

The whole *Magnalia* is a Wonder Book—of monsters, but much more of miracles and saints; and it is only when one escapes from its spell that one reflects that everything in the little world of the Massachusetts Bay Colony and its Holy City of Boston is magnified to the proportions of the epic or the marvelous. Can every actor have been so heroically noble, so learned, so pious? Can God's whole attention—as well as Satan's—have been given to what happened in Massachusetts?

Yes, in a sense, it can have been, for the real New England is not a geographical area but a Holy State. If the visible New England has been long in the economic and political hands of 'aliens,' long now a combination of academic institutions and summer resorts, still, the 'real New England' was always a Platonic Idea or a Biblical myth, like Paradise before it was lost. Van Wyck Brooks can speak of the Holy State as having a "Flowering" and an "Indian Summer"; but to the New England mind, which is nothing if not critical, New England began its Fall as soon as it began to exist.

Indeed, Thomas Hooker, founder of the Hartford colony, ominously said as he took ship for New England, "Farewell, England! I expect now no more to see that religious zeal and power of godliness which I have seen among professors [i.e., the professing Christian Puritans] in that land." And, adds Mather, Hooker "had sagacious and prophetical apprehensions of the declensions which would attend 'reforming churches' when they came to enjoy a place of liberty. He said 'that adversity had slain its thousands, but prosperity would slay its ten thousands.' "

These are ominous words about the failure of success, but none the less painfully true. And they partly explain Mather's own forebodings and relinquishments: in the "General Introduction" to the *Magnalia* he is willing to believe that the "migration of thousands of reformers into the retirements of an American desert" was to give to the world a "specimen of the many good things that He would have His churches elsewhere aspire and arise unto. And this being done, He knows whether there be not all done that New England was planted for, and whether the plantation may not soon after this come to nothing. . . . But whether New England may live elsewhere or not it must live in our history!"

This last exclamatory sentence reverberates in the memory. Detached from its context, it is susceptible of wide interpretation; but in its place on Mather's page, it is an expression at once of defiance, despair, and pride. "Our" is not the imperial or auctorial pronoun. Throughout the "General Introduction," Mather writes of himself in the at once more egotistic and more modest first person singular: when he speaks of his own *Magnalia*, he calls it "my Church History." "We" and "our" refer to the orthodox Puritans of the Bay Colony; and "our history" is the history unwritten or written, though especially written, of the New England Puritans of the seventeenth century, for whom, in reverential retrospect, Mather is the spokesman. He is, to be sure, included in the "we," but primarily as a member of the orthodox community, and only secondarily as the proud spokesman. And throughout the *Magnalia*, "our" (the Latin *noster*) keeps appearing (as by stylistic contagion it does in this essay) to mean "one of ours" of whom we are proud: "our Hooker," "our Eliot," "our Scholasticus."

In Mather's judgment, New England Religion is likely the closest return ever made to the first and Golden Age of Christianity, to return to which, he asserts, "will make a man a Protestant, and, I may add, a Puritan." So signal an experiment may fail; the Theocracy (the word is not Mather's but the concept is) may become extinct in its place, as Mather correctly saw it about to become. But the experiment will (like other Utopias) pass into history, the memorable parts of the past; and there it will survive, for future admiration and emulation. The real New England is an Idea and a Model.

That the Idea may survive, it is of course important that the New England experiment be written down; and hence the need for the *Magnalia*. To tell "our history" is the burden laid upon "my history"; and after his quoted sentence Mather enters upon a celebration of history writing, especially that of the Church historians like Luke (whose Gospel and Book of Acts have "given us more glorious entertainments" than Thucydides, Polybius, and Tacitus)—like "our own English writers," Baker, Heylin, and Fuller.

III

Should a reader come to Mather's book supposing it to be a history of New England, he would be surprised at the meager space, information, and interest its author gives to the physical adventures of the Pilgrims and the Puritans, matters which Governor Bradford treats with such dignified and yet detailed concern. The word 'wilderness,' which in Bradford is so literally real, is, for Mather, who often uses it, a ritual word connoting the ectypal relation of the flight of the New England Puritans from their Laudian persecutors to the wanderings of the archetypal Israel, escaping from Egypt to the Promised Land.

But our book is plainly called an 'ecclesiastical history': the polity, the politics, the founding of the college, and the warfare of New England are but means to the establishment and preservation of a thoroughly reformed Church of Christ. As Mather observes, the creation of the world is described by Moses in two chapters of Genesis, while the prescriptions for the building and ritual of the Tabernacle (in Deuteronomy and Leviticus) take something like seven times as many chapters. And the great John Cotton himself, Mather's revered grandfather, was responsible for the Bay Colony's establishment of a 'Theocracy' in which "none should be electors nor elected . . . except such as were visible subjects of our Lord Jesus Christ, personally confederated in our churches. . . ."

Important and great as were New England's governors, then, they held but secondary rank in comparison with the learned and godly clergy, the interpreters of the Sacred Scriptures, the "oracles of God," which provided full instructions for both civil and ecclesiastical order. And much the most copious and memorable part of the *Magnalia* is the Third Book, "De Viris Illustribus . . . Containing the Lives of near Fifty Divines considerable in the Churches of New-England."

The greatest of these were the immigrant clergy, most of them educated at that nursery of Puritanism, Emmanuel College, Cambridge, and most of them already men of eminence and influence in their native land. Emigrating commonly in middle life, they brought with them their habits of hard study, constant self-examination, addiction to much and long preaching (two substantial sermons on Sunday with another substantial sermon, called a 'lecture,' for delivery on a weekday). They had the power of men who have struggled to attain their convictions and sacrificed to preserve them.

These 'fifty lives' are the lives of saints—saints who combine the Aaronic priesthood with Elijah's "school of prophets" (a favorite name for Harvard College). Almost without exception, they were married: sometimes, like Mather himself, three times; and they often married clerical widows or the daughters of clergymen. Mather's grandfather Richard, after the death of his first wife, married "the pious widow of the most famous John Cotton." Richard's youngest son by his first wife, the celebrated Increase, married Mrs. Mather's daughter, Maria Cotton; and from this marriage was born the author of the *Magnalia*. But Richard Mather "gave the church no less than four sons to be worthy ministers of the gospel." To have clerical sons, and daughters who had married clerical sons-in-law, was a proud joy to the Puritan ministers.

Rare indeed was the unmarried clergyman, so rare that when Mather writes the life of Thomas Parker, "Scholasticus," he has to explain that his subject meditated marriage but was at the time so assaulted with doubts about the truth of Scripture that, turning to Scripture prophecies and their fulfillment in order to assure his faith, he forgot about marrying; then to equate the pupils whom Parker did have with the sons he didn't; and lastly to pronounce, ambiguously but eloquently, of his death, that he "went to the immortals . . . after he had lived all his days a single man": that, having spent "a great part of his days engaged in apocalyptic studies," he "went unto the apocalyptical virgins who 'follow the Lamb whithersoever he goes.' "

Mather's clerical biographies differ widely in length, according to the importance of his subject, the amount of information to be had, or (conceivably) the biographer's degree of interest, but, despite the differences in scale, a general ideal pattern for the 'saint's life' can be discerned. It will include the saint's ancestry; his conversion, from sin or Anglicanism or both; his marriages and their offspring; his studies—less his formal education than his life-long habit; his mode and method of preaching; his books, if he published; quotation from his "reserved"—his unpublished and indeed private—papers, diaries, journals, and 'resolutions' (those injunctions to self of which Jonathan Edwards', in the following century, are an eminent example); his characteristic sayings; and, finally, the circumstances of his death and his dying counsels—what Mather generically calls *Apothegmata morientum*.

Three of these topics shall be illustrated by extracts: studies, preaching, and dying words. The first two ever interested Mather, for they were his own favorite occupations and his grounds for glory; and, with little translation, they interest any academic humanist or other member of the group which Coleridge called the "clerisy"—the socially functioning and responsible intellectuals. As for 'last words,' I shall confess that not only do I share Mather's fondness for recording the habitual and characteristic sayings of wise men, what they were "wont to say" (such as the Jews have rightly preserved in the *Pirke Abot*, or *Sayings of the Fathers*), but that I am also willing to receive as pious representative fictions the recorded, or attributed, and certainly always generously interpreted, final overheard utterances.

The proper epitaph for a New England clergyman requires, before the proper name and the office, two epithets— pious and learned. Richard Mather, Cotton's grandfather, was "a very hard student." The morning before he died, he begged his friends to lead him from his "lodging room" into his study; and, when they could not, he said, "I see I am not able; I have not been in my study several days; and is it not a lamentable thing that I should lose so much time?" Indeed, the last two years of his life he suffered from that scourge of the sedentary, "namely, the stone, which proved to be the tombstone whereby all his labors and sorrows were *in fine* brought unto a period."

Mather's other and more celebrated grandfather, the Reverend John Cotton, "the father and glory of Boston," was an indefatigable student who "went not much abroad"—outside of his house and his church. "Twelve hours a day he commonly studied, and would call that 'a scholar's day'. . . ." In consequence, he was "a most universal scholar and a living system of the liberal arts and a walking library." He could talk in Hebrew, and Latin he both wrote and spoke.

Mather's younger brother Nathaniel, who died in youth, "afforded not so much a pattern as a caution to young students," for, "while he thus devoured books, it came to pass that books devoured him. . . ." Together with his other attainments he had "no small measure of Rabbinic learning."

'Rabbinic learning' occupied a surprisingly important part in early Harvard College; indeed, the eminent historian of seventeenth-century Harvard, finds "the most distinctive feature" of its curriculum to be the "emphasis on Hebrew and kindred languages." The reason appears partially to have been the view of great scholars such as Selden and Theophilus Gale that Hebrew was the *Ursprache* of all European tongues; partly the marked Puritan emphasis upon the Old Testament; partly the fact that it was the favorite subject of the two great presidents of the century, the Reverends Henry Dunster and Charles Chauncy. Dunster wrote a learned Friend to send him "whatsoever Hebrew, Caldee, Syriack, or Arabick authors" he could procure. And Theophilus Gale, who died in 1678, bequeathed something like a thousand volumes of Targums, Talmuds, and other Rabbinical literature to Harvard.

Thomas Thatcher, one of Mather's saints, was "a most incomparable scribe"; "There are yet extant monuments of Syriac and other Oriental characters of his writings which are hardly to be imitated." Samuel Newman, the *Bibliander Nov-Anglicus,*" was a maker of Biblical concordances—a genre of which Mather gives a lengthy history, including the great names of Rabbi Isaac Nathan, Origen, Robert and Henry Stephens; yet, says he, Newman made a "more elaborate concordance of the Bible than had ever yet been seen in Europe"; and after he migrated to New England, he made it "yet more elaborate." The "immoderate studies" of Thomas Parker, our "*Scholasticus,*" caused damage to both his eyes—a torment to a scholar which he bore patiently, saying to himself, "Well, they'll be restored shortly at the resurrection."

The Protestant—the Puritan—Sabbath exists for, centers in, the sermon; and it is almost, but not quite, true that learning and study exist that the sermon, though concealing its learning and its art, shall be possessed of both; for the Puritans did not conceive of the sermon as the Pentecostal outflow, the spontaneous effusion, of a man possibly pious but certainly uneducated.

The great apostle to the Indians, John Eliot, the most patently radiant of Mather's saints, "liked no preaching but what had been well studied for; and he would very much commend a sermon which he could perceive had required some good thinking and reading in the author of it." After the sermon preached by another (for holy Eliot listened to the sermons of others as well as to his own), he said, "Brother, there was oil required for the service of the sanctuary; but it must be beaten oil [Exod. 27:20; Lev. 24:2]. I praise God that I saw your oil so well beaten today; the Lord help us always by good study to beat our oil that there may be no knots in our sermons left undissolved and that there may a clear light be thereby given in the house of God."

The great Thomas Hooker's advice to young ministers was that "they would with careful study preach over the whole book of divinity methodically": that is, instead of following the Church Year (which, including Christmas and Easter, the Puritans rejected), the congregation was to be given a series of systematic discourses on the chief topics of Christian theology.

This methodical preaching, which goes down to the time of Edwards and his disciples, and which was undoubtedly the norm, admitted of deviation. The original scheme for the New England system appears to have postulated what was possible only for large, chiefly city, churches: that there should be two clergymen, one called the teacher, or doctrinal instructor, and the other the pastor.

The First Church of Boston had such in Mr. Cotton and Mr. Wilson; and Mather remarks that, before their joint ministry, Wilson "had been used unto a more methodical way of preaching . . . ; but after he became pastor . . . he gave himself a liberty to preach more after the primitive manner—without any distinct propositions, but chiefly in exhortations and admonitions and good wholesome counsels tending to excite *good motions* in the minds of his hearers (but upon the same texts that were doctrinally handled by his colleague instantly before . . .)."

Wilson, like Eliot, was evidently a Johannine and not a

Pauline Puritan—orthodox, to be sure, but distinguished primarily by humility, tenderness, prayer, and love—an aged John of the Epistles, to whom "the most considerable people in the country" came from far that he might give their children his "patriarchal benedictions."

Of Eliot's "way of Preaching," Mather (in the masterpiece of his 'Saints' lives') says: "It was food and not froth which in his *public* sermons he entertained the souls of his people with; he did not starve them with empty and windy speculations. . . . His way of preaching was very plain; so that the very lambs might wade into his discourses on those texts and themes wherein elephants might swim. . . ." Such a man, a "good man," as even William Carlos Williams parenthetically admits during his diatribe against the Puritans in *The American Grain*, might even reach those 'praying Indians' whom the French Catholics much more abundantly converted.

When Mather speaks of the Apostle's "public sermons," the implied distinction is reasonably clear. Eliot preached also by his life and prayers and his conversations; he ever edified. When he heard any news of importance, his usual response was "Brethren, let us turn all this into a prayer." And, "though sufficiently pleasant and witty in company—he was affable and facetious rather than morose in conversation," he raised ever "some holy observation" on whatever might be the theme of discussion. And (like Mather himself), he had "a particular art at spiritualizing of earthly objects." Accordingly, when he walked, rather feeble and weary, up Roxbury's Meetinghouse Hill, he said to his companion, "This is very like the way to heaven: 't is up hill! The Lord by his grace fetch us up," and then, seeing a nearby bush, added, "and truly there are thorns and briars in the way, too."

If to the dying words of a humanist some representative or symbolic meaning is attached—as when Lord Chesterfield, the "ruling passion strong in death," shows his politeness by saying, "Show the gentleman a chair," and as when Goethe utters, "Light, more light," as when Thoreau murmurs, "Moose —Indians," how much more importance must be assigned to the dying words of a saint, before whose vision the Gates of Paradise must already begin to open.

The *"vulgar error* of the signal sweetness in the song of a dying swan was a very truth in our expiring Eliot; his last breath smelt strong of Heaven, and was articulated to none but very gracious notes, one of the last whereof was, 'Welcome, Joy,' and at last it went away calling upon the standers-by to 'Pray, pray, pray'. . . ." The evening before the Reverend John Wilson, pastor of Boston, died, his daughter asked him, "Sir, how do you do?" He held up his hand and said, "Vanishing things! Vanishing things!" The Reverend Samuel Newman was heard to say, " 'And now, ye angels of the Lord Jesus Christ, come, do your office,' with which words he immediately expired his holy soul into the arms of angels. . . ." Even a 'priest's wife' might utter as her dying words, as did Thomas Thatcher's first wife, "Come, Lord Jesus, come quickly, Why are Thy chariot-wheels so long a-coming?"—a delicate blend of Rev. 22:12 and 2 Kings 2:11–12.

The really sensitive use of the Bible in the writings and sayings of the Pilgrims and Puritans is manifest not when they quote *verbatim*, text affixed, but when—as in this prayer, and in the *History* of Governor Bradford—one phrase and another come to their Book-saturated minds, when the assumption of a common authoritative mythology is so natural as to make either marks of quotation or a reference to the text as insulting to others as unnatural to them.

IV

Stylistically, the *Magnalia* is probably the latest example of Baroque prose in English, as Edward Taylor's *Meditations* is the latest Baroque poetry. This belatedness may partly be explained by the authors' Colonial setting: shifts of taste used to migrate more slowly than they do now, and they move more slowly in the provinces and colonies than in Paris and London.

But in the former case, at least, the situation is more complex. For one thing, Mather was basically a conservative, the defender of what he calls "the Good Old Way." The grandson of the two eminent Puritans whose names were coupled in his, he had claims to importance which were partly hereditary. Politically, socially, and theologically, he believed himself to represent the traditional orthodox views of his ancestors and the other founding fathers of New England.

For another thing, Mather's chief talents were of a sort out of keeping with those lauded and fostered by the age of the Restoration into which he was born—the age of Common Sense, Rationalism, Neoclassicism—the age dominated by Descartes, Locke, and Newton, literarily by Addison, Pope, and Swift. He was a man, to be sure, of encyclopedic interests—among which he included scientific observations of the simpler sort and some concern for 'Natural Philosophy' and its reconciliation with 'Revealed Religion.' But his central talents were for learning of an old-fashioned kind—rather for accumulation and erudition than scholarly methodology, for wit and fancy (in Addison's terminology, mostly 'false wit'), and for similes and metaphors, whether aggrandizing (like the Biblical and classical similes he applies to his New England 'Worthies') or grotesque. It would be painful, and probably futile, for a man so endowed to constrict himself to a thinner epistemology and aesthetic. But, happily, he believed his causes, though out of fashion, to be right; and he did not, fundamentally, attempt to adapt himself and his style to the dominant modes of his time.

Some adaptation Mather certainly made in his writing; but it was adaptation not to the times but to his subject and his audience—to the *genre* in which he was working. So there are differences in his style between his sermons (which aim at a plainer style and a more systematic arrangement), his 'political fables' (in the mode of the Age of Anne), his *Christian Philosopher,* and his *Essays to Do Good* (essays appropriately praised by Dr. Franklin), his scientific communications, and his *Magnalia.*

According to his theory of *decorum,* or generic adaptation, Mather used in the *Magnalia,* especially in the "General Introduction," the Baroque, for him the 'grand' or epic style. In this book, Church History was his *genre* and his subject, a subject of such dignity as suitably to evoke elaboration and ornamentation; and he was writing not *ad populum* but *ad clerum*, for scholars and clergymen, and not primarily for his parishioners and other fellow countrymen but for the learned Protestants of England (where his book was, by design, published) and of Europe.

In a history, a prose form with its likeness to the epic, Mather needed not to practice the celebrated 'plain style' of his grandfathers (whose sermons he commends for their conscious plainness), the style resumed in the sermons and treatises of President Edwards; nor did he need to follow the counsel of the masters of the Puritans, Perkins and Ames, that the preacher, though possessed of erudition, should conceal it as unedifying to his auditors. In this, his designedly great work, a work primarily of celebration, he was free to display his learning and wit, his allusiveness, his taste for abrupt turns of style, for anecdotes and apothegms. He may well have had in mind Thomas Fuller's *Church History of England* as he wrote his of New England. It is certainly books like Fuller's *History* and *Worthies* and Burton's *Anatomy of Melancholy* which are the prototypes of the *Magnalia*—books of learning, wit, anecdotes, and moralizings. The mode of the book is of the first half of the seventeenth century.

Mather published his book in 1702, when he was still under forty. When, in 1723, he died, the minister of the Old South Church, preaching a funeral sermon abundant in encomia, admitted the style of the deceased to be "something singular, and not so agreeable to the *gust* of the age." Of this discrepancy Mather was aware. Some critics, he says in his "Introduction," "will reckon the style embellished with too much ornament, by the multiplied references to other and former concerns, closely couched, for the observation of the attentive, in almost every paragraph. . . ." He attempted to palliate his offense by explaining his "embellishments" were not at second-hand, drawn from other men's anthologies, and that he had not labored to insert them; that they were, on the contrary, "choice flowers . . . almost unavoidably putting

themselves into the author's hand while about his work . . . ,"
a statement which (with its delightful "almost") I suppose to
be literally or legally true, for he does not assert that he quotes
from memory, capacious though his memory was. Like every
good seventeenth-century scholar, or indeed man of letters, he
kept commonplace books; and, remembering the extracts he
had copied, he saw but intelligent thrift in looking them up
and using them.

Baroquely, Mather delights in displaying his erudition,
certainly rich. He learned, for missionary purposes, to read
and write in French, Spanish, and even in one of the many
Amerind tongues; but his authorities are Hebrew, Greek, and
Latin; and within the scope of those learned tongues his range
is great. That no modern edition of his Work has been issued
is perhaps the less surprising when one thinks how many writers and scholars eminent in his day have been forgotten and
now require scholarly annotation.

Throughout the *Magnalia*, certainly, the erudition is un-
failing: in the Greek Fathers of the Church, in the Talmudic
Rabbis, in the theologians and scholars of the Reformed
Churches. Writing of young Shepard's "secret-fasts," he cites
the "commendations given to fasting by Basil and Cyprian in
their orations about it, and by Ambrose in his book of Elias
. . . the words of Chrysostom concerning this duty. . . ." And
the Talmud is yet more frequently cited and quoted than the
Greek Fathers—most commonly in Latin.

At the end of his elaborately figured 'Introduction,'
Mather says that he will now introduce "The fathers of New-
England without the least fiction or flower of rhetoric," giving
their descendants but the "plain history" of their lives. We
need have no fear of the promise being kept.

Our author has no distaste for the minor forms of Baroque
wit. He does not repudiate the pious anagrams of which the
Puritans—in New England, especially Mr. Wilson—were fond;
and, though citing the Alexandrian Lycophron, reminds us
that "They who affect such grammatical curiosities will be
willing to plead a prescription of much and higher and elder

antiquity" for them—"even the *temurah* or *mutation* with which the Jews do *criticize* upon the oracles of the Old Testament. 'There,' they say, 'you'll find the anagrams of our first father's name *Haadam* to express *Adamah*, the name of the earth, whence he had his origin.' "

Mather delighted in the metaphorizing of proper names. When John Cotton came to Boston, there were two other eminent ministers with him in the ship, Mr. Hooker and Mr. Stone, so that "the poor people in the wilderness" of New England were reported to have said that now they had answer for their "three great necessities: Cotton for their clothing, Hooker for their fishing; and Stone for their building."

Indeed, for purposes of edification and pious fancy, Mather could use every kind of name at all promising: the Christian name, the surname; even the antonym of the surname. Three examples:

Jesus found St. Philip, and said to him "Follow me," and Philip went in search of his brother who was resting under a fig tree. Upon this Mather, beginning his life of Nathanael Rogers, gives what he calls "a reflection, carrying in it somewhat of curiosity. . . . At the beginning of the Law under the Old Testament, you have Nature in our Adam under a tree; at the beginning of the Gospel under the New Testament [John 1:48], you have Grace under a tree in Nathanael." Adam Blackman prompts the antonymic reflection that this holy man, notwithstanding his name, was, for his holiness, "A Nazarite purer than snow, whiter than milk." Of Samuel Whiting, who bore the surname of a fish: "The ecclesiastical sharks then drove this Whiting over the *Atlantic* ocean unto the American strand . . . ," Yet our Whiting "would have thought himself out of his element if he had ever been at any time anywhere but in the *Pacific* ocean." To a truly Baroque *gust*, this last is assuredly a pardonable pun.

Mather's fancy does not fail him even when the saint's name provides no happy hint. In his life of Richard Denton, a page developing the conceit of clouds with the aid of all manner of Scriptural clouds, the occasion for the figure is almost concealed in the middle of the page-long eulogium; and the hint is the *rumor* that he was blind of one eye, that his vision was partially clouded. That possibility is enough to warrant the tesselation of a mosaic.

"The apostle describing the false ministers of those primitive times, he calls them 'clouds without water, carried about of winds.' As for the true ministers of our primitive times, they were indeed 'carried about of Winds': though not the winds of strange doctrines, yet the winds of hard suffering did carry them as far as from Europe into America. . . . But they came; they came with showers of blessing."

Whatever the state of his ocularity, Denton was "far from cloudy in his conceptions and principles of divinity, whereof he wrote a system . . ." ; and last he got into Heaven, "beyond clouds and the clouds of heaven. . . ."

When, in 1726, the year before he died, Mather published his *Manuductio ad Ministerium,* or Advice to Clerical Candidates, he took cognizance of the shift in style from the Baroque to the Neoclassical with a spirited defense of his own. Up to a point, he concedes tolerance, will allow that every man has a right to his own style, as he has to his own characteristic way of walking, his "gait"—though in that case Mather too has a right to his. But he does not concede that there are not better ways and worse, or thinner and richer. However much "fashion and humor may prevail," indolent, easy writers "must not think that the club at their coffee-house is all the world." Even if "a more massy way of writing," one of solid erudition and abundant fancy, "be never so much *disgusted* at this day, a better *gust* will come on."

A "better gust" began to return with the Romantics, both in England and America—a turn back from Neoclassicism to the Baroque (the 'Metaphysical,' as it was Englishly called). Lamb and Coleridge, who delighted in Fuller and Burton, would doubtless, had they known it, taken pleasure in the *Magnalia*. Among our own New England Romantics, the *Magnalia* was known and cherished, not for its style (pleasure in which has been reserved for our own Baroque-oriented time) but for its mythic quality and power. This power has been attested to by its author's most recent judge and one of his most acute: "For two centuries and even longer, Americans, even those who criticized the *Magnalia* or professed to despise its author, have seen the great struggle for New England's soul through Cotton Mather's eyes." It is difficult to deny the gift of imagination to a historian who thus makes centuries of other men see through his eyes.

v

Mather's mind moved in a world of allusions and of images, not visual images from the world immediately about him but metaphors and emblems, 'conceits.' The tangible reminds him of his reading and his vigils. Unlike his father, he never went far from Boston. But, like Robert Burton, he traveled by map and chronicle, translating all into his own nostalgic and literary substance. Perhaps it is correct to say, too, that he was the first of that long line of New Englanders who have looked back to the glories of the forefathers and the pristine purity of the Idea of New England. Like subsequent Bostonians, he continued to try to save Boston, Massachusetts, New England, the world. He labored against his sense of vanished glory by essays to do good, projects for improving this and that, philanthropic enterprises large and futile or useful but petty; meanwhile his inner self was absorbed in the magnified wonders of the past and the millennial wonders to come.

So he seems to have appeared to Hawthorne, who knew his writings well. In *Grandfather's Chair*, his 'child's history' of New England, he represents Dr. Mather sitting in his study; he cites the inscription over its portal, "Be Brief," his warning to visitors not needlessly to interrupt this great man's "wonderful labors" on the Wonder Book. The *Magnalia* is that "strange, pedantic history, in which true events and real personages move before the reader with the dreamy aspect which they wore in Cotton Mather's singular mind."

1964

The Scarlet Letter

In structure, *The Scarlet Letter* is rather a monody, like
Wuthering Heights (its closest English analogue for intensity)
or *The Spoils of Poynton* (with its thematic concentration),
than like the massively rich and contrapuntal Victorian novel
—say *Middlemarch* or *Bleak House*. And, conducted almost
entirely in dialogues between two persons, or in tableaux, with
something like the Greek chorus in the commenting community, it is also much nearer to a tragedy of Racine's than to the
Elizabethan drama, of which the three-volumed Victorian
novel was the legitimate successor.

This purity of method, this structural condensation and
concentration, prime virtues of *The Scarlet Letter*, disturbed,
while they obsessed, its author. He regretted not being able to
intersperse the gloom of his novel by some chapters, episodes,
or passages in a lighter mode. "Keeping so close to its point as
the tale does, and diversified no otherwise than by turning different sides of the same idea to the reader's mind," he wrote
his publisher, would, he feared, bore, disgust, or otherwise
alienate the reader.

But the enduring power of the book lies in its "keeping so
close to its point," lies in its method: looking at the "same
idea" (the situation or theme) from "different sides." Hawthorne's phrase, "different sides," is not synonymous with the
Jamesian "point of view," though there is a degree of overlap.
Hawthorne is the nineteenth-century omniscient author; and it
is he who shows us the "different sides," now a character's

public behavior, now the same character's private introspection; who presents two characters operating on each other; who gives us the shifting attitudes of the community to the actions of the central figures; who provides settings and symbols and generalizing comments. It is none the less true that the author does not flit from character to character. Each chapter has not only a center of interest, commonly indicated by its title, but tends to be seen through a single or central consciousness. As we remember the novel, the interpolations and other deviations fall away, and we retain the impression of a massive construction in terms of centers of interest and of consciousness.

The first eight chapters of the novel are seen through Hester's consciousness; even though the minister appears from time to time it is in his public capacity as her "pastor." The next four concern the minister, two of them close studies of "The Interior of a [Dimmesdale's] Heart." Hester again engages the next four. The Forest chapters represent the only real meeting, the only real converse between the two.

This is an eminently proper mode of telling the story. The two characters are joined by an act which occurred before the novel opens. They never meet again save twice, ritualistically, on the scaffold, and once, rituals dispensed with, in the Forest. Otherwise, these are tales of two isolated characters, isolated save for the attendant spirit of each—Pearl for Hester; for Dimmesdale, Chillingworth. Hester's story, as that of sin made public, must begin the novel; the telling of Dimmesdale's, as that of sin concealed, must be delayed till its effects, however ambivalently interpreted, begin to show. The last chapters must present both characters to our consciousness, even though Dimmesdale recedes into something like the public figure of the early chapters, lost in his double role of preacher and dying confessor.

The composition of the novel, deeply as it stirred Hawthorne, was creatively easy, for (as he wrote his publisher), "all being all in one tone, I had only to get my pitch and could then go on interminably." But this high, or deep, tragic pitch made him uncomfortable—as, I dare say, did Melville's praise of his *Mosses from an Old Manse,* in which the new friend, who was beginning to write *Moby Dick,* spoke of "the blackness in Hawthorne . . . that so fixes and fascinates me," singling out from that collection "Young Goodman Brown," a piece "as deep as Dante." Hawthorne, waiving the question of his 'best,' preferred *The House of the Seven Gables* as "more characteristic" of him than *The Scarlet Letter;* and doubtless among his tales, too, he would have preferred the "more characteristic" to the 'best.' A critic may be pardoned if he prefers the 'best.'

And certainly *The Scarlet Letter* resumes, develops, and concentrates the themes which Hawthorne had already essayed in some of his chief and greatest short stories—"Roger Malvin's Burial," "The Minister's Black Veil," and, especially, "Young Goodman Brown": concealment of sin, penance, and penitence; the distinction between the comparatively lighter sins of passion and the graver sins of cold blood—pride, calculated revenge; the legacy of sin in making one detect, or suspect, it in others.

II

In reading Hawthorne's masterpiece, one should be careful to distinguish the 'story,' 'fable,' or 'myth' from the author's commentary. Even in his own lifetime, the now forgotten but good Boston critic, E. P. Whipple, wrote, acutely, that Hawthorne's "great books appear not so much created by him as through him. They have the character of revelations,—he, the instrument, being often troubled with the burden they impose upon his mind." *The Scarlet Letter* seems preeminently such a case. The 'myth' was a delivery; the commentary was an offering.

The novelist, whether the later James of the strict point of view constructions, or Jane Austen and E. M. Forster and Dostoevski, has an enviable 'dramatic' privilege. If his characters act out their willed destiny and utter the views appropriate to their characters, the novelist (who is also a nonwriter, a man whose divided self approves but in part of what his *personae* say and do) has the immunity of dissociating himself from a position which he can empathize or entertain but to which he does not wish to commit himself. Hawthorne could, if necessary, let his latent 'moral'—that of his powerfully presented 'myth'—go one way while he safeguarded his other self by uttering, in his own person, words of warning or reproof.

What the author says through his characters cannot 'legally' be quoted as his attitude; but, on the other hand, what he says as commentator must, almost equally, be regarded as not the view of his total self. As commentator, he may say what he thinks he believes or what is prudential. The blessed immunity and gift, thus, is to be able to give voice to all the voices in him, not, finally, attempting to suppress any of them—not, finally, feeling the need to pull himself together into the tight doctrinal consistency at which a theologian or philosopher must aim.

One cannot, in *The Scarlet Letter*, take 'proof-texts' out of their context or utterances away from their speakers. Hence, the 'moral' of the novel is not contained, as an eminent critic once asserted, in Hester's avowal to her "pastor" in the pagan Forest, that "What we did had a consecration of its own." Nor, since so many morals can be drawn from Dimmesdale's misery, are we to think that they can be summed up in the novelist's choice from among them, "Be true! Be true! Be true!" Because there are, in Hawthorne's phrase (doubtless half-ironic, half-satiric of Sunday School books and tracts), "many morals," the book has no 'moral.' At the least, half-true, and importantly true, is Henry James's conception that it was not as a 'moralist' that Hawthorne was drawn to his tales and novels of sin, that "What pleased him in such subjects was their picturesquesness, their rich duskiness of color, their chiaroscuro. . . ."

Certainly, his literary fascination with sin was quite as much aesthetic and psychological as moral. As Henry, brother of William, so truly says of Hawthorne, "he cared for the deeper psychology." Such comparatives as "deeper" left suspended without what they are "deeper" than, I dislike; but I can't pretend, at least in this instance, not to know what is meant: deeper than analysis of manners, deeper than consciousness, deeper than normal normality—deeper also than 'univalent' judgments. Ambivalence and plurivalence are the "deeper psychology" open to the novelist even when, speaking in his own person, he too, casts a vote: I do not want to say a 'decisive vote,' since I doubt that, as commentator, his 'view' of his own work has any more authority than that of another critic: it may even have less.

III

Two of the characters in *The Scarlet Letter* certainly engaged Hawthorne in his 'deeper psychology,' and are richly developed.

About Hester, her creator had—as he did about his other brunettes, Zenobia and Miriam—ambivalent feelings. Twice, in *The Scarlet Letter*, he compares her to that seventeenth-century feminist Anne Hutchinson, whom, in *Grandfather's Chair*, his chronicle of New England history written for children, he calls, half or more than half ironically, "saintly"—that is, she who was regarded by many as saintly. 'Strong' women, whether sirens, seers, or reformers, were not, in his judgment, womanly.

For Hester, he provides some Catholic similitudes—the most striking in the description of her first appearance on the scaffold. "Had there been a Papist among the crowd of Puritans, he might have seen . . . an object to remind him of Divine Maternity . . ." But it would have reminded him, indeed, "only by contrast, of that sacred image of sinless motherhood, whose infant was to redeem the world. Here . . . the world was only the darker for this woman's beauty, and the more lost for the infant that she bore."

And, again: after seven years, Hester's life of charity gave her "scarlet letter the effect of the cross on a nun's breast." But Hawthorne draws back from taking the view which her life of self-abnegation might seem to entitle her to receive and him to take; for such a view would be based on Hester's Stoic pride and courage, not on her inner life of motive and thought. She has, to be sure, done penance, and done it with dignity—but she has done it with a *proud* dignity, for she is not penitent.

Her rich and luxuriant hair, though closely hidden by her cap, has not been cropped. Seven years after her act of adultery she still believes that what she and her lover did had "a consecration of its own." It is one of Hawthorne's shrewdest insights and axioms that "persons who speculate the most boldly often conform with the most perfect quietude to the external regulations of society. The thought suffices them. . . ." And so Hester, outwardly penitent and charitable, allowed herself "a freedom of speculation which our forefathers, had they known of it, would have held to be a deadlier crime than that stigmatized by the scarlet letter." Some of these doubts and theorizings concerned the position of woman; and Hawthorne, antifeminist that he was, says of Hester that, her heart having lost its "regular and healthy throb," she "wandered without a clew in the dark labyrinth of mind. . . ."

Hester has her femininities: her loyalty to her lover and to her child and the love of her craft ("Her Needle"). But her needle, like her mind, shows something awry. For Hawthorne bestows upon her—a kinswoman in this respect to Zenobia and Miriam—a "rich, voluptuous, Oriental characteristic." Despite her self-imposed penances of making "coarse garments for the poor"—gifts to those poor who often but revile and insult her, she allows her fancy and needleship free play in designing clothes for Pearl, her "elf-child."

Even more signally, she shows, in the badge of shame she herself wears—and that from her first appearance on the scaffold—a pride triumphing over her shame. It does not pass unnoticed by the women spectators at the scaffold: one remarks that the adulteress has made "a pride" out of what her judges meant for a punishment. And "at her needle," though clad in her gray robe of coarsest material, Hester still wears on her breast, "in the curiously embroidered letter, a specimen of her delicate and imaginative skill, of which the dames of a court might gladly have availed themselves. . . ."

Appropriate as it is for the pious Bostonians to think Hester a witch, Hester has not signed with her own scarlet blood the Devil's book. Better, from an orthodox Puritan stance, that she had done so. But she has by-passed all that. She belongs in the Forest, where, in the one recorded conversation between the Pastor and his Parishioner, she meets Dimmesdale; she belongs in the Forest not because it is the Devil's opposing citadel to the Town but because she is pagan—as we might now say, because she is a 'naturalist.' To the Forest she belongs as does "the wild Indian." For years she "has looked from this estranged point of view at human institutions"—human, not merely Puritan—"criticizing all—with hardly more reverence than an Indian would feel for the clerical bands" (the prenineteenth century equivalent of the priest's collar), "the judicial robe, the pillory, the gallows, the fireside" (wedded, domestic, and familial bliss), "or the church."

"Like the wild Indian" (Hawthorne is in no danger of saying or thinking of the 'noble savage'), Hester has not judged men by their professional vestments or their status, nor institutions by virtue of their ideal rank in the hierarchy of some philosopher like Plato or Edmund Burke.

That her judgment was thus disillusioned was both good and bad: indeed, there are two seemingly contradictory truths both of which must be asserted and maintained. One is respect for persons in their representative capacities; for church, state, and university represent, with varying degrees of adequacy, the Ideas of holiness, civic virtue, and learning. The other is a dispassionately critical judgment which distinguishes between the personal and institutional representatives of the Ideas and the Ideas themselves. A third, doubtless, is the dispassionately critical judgment as to when particular persons and particular institutions so inadequately represent their respective Ideas as no longer to be sufferable—to require reform, expulsion, substitution; this is the Revolutionary judgment.

The difficulty of keeping these three truths—or even the

first two of them—before one's mind in steady equipoise is as difficult as it is necessary. Hawthorne never attempted to formulate explicitly, even briefly, what I have just said; but such a conception seems clearly implicit in his characterization of Hester. Hester has been taught by shame, despair, and solitude; but, though they "had made her strong," that had "taught her much amiss."

Hester's exemplary conduct in the years which follow her first scene on the scaffold must be interpreted not as penitence but as stoicism, especially, a stoical disdain for the 'views' of society. She is bound to her Boston bondage partly by a kind of instinctive or romantic fatalism—not of the theological kind but fatalism of being bound to the place where she 'sinned' and to her lover. I put the word 'sinned' in quotes because Hester has not repented, not thinking that she has done anything of which she should repent. She still loves Dimmesdale, or at any event pities him, as weaker than herself; and, upon Dimmesdale's appeal to her, when (by her design and his accident) they meet in the Forest, that she advise him what to do, she is immediately purposeful and practical. Let him go into the forest among the Indians, or back to England, or to Europe. She is imperative: "Preach! Write! act! Do anything save to lie down and die!" Chillingworth's persecutions have made him too "feeble to will and to do"—will soon leave him "powerless even to repent! Up, and away!" And she arranges passage to England on a ship soon to leave Boston.

After Dimmesdale's death, Hester and Pearl disappear—Pearl, 'for good,' Hester, for many years. Yet Hester finally returns to Boston and to her gray cottage and her gray robe and her scarlet letter, for "Here had been her sin; her sorrow; and here was yet to be her penitence." The "yet to be," ambiguous in isolation, seems, in the rest of the penultimate paragraph, to mean that at the end of her life she did repent. In part, at least, this repentance was her renunciation of her earlier fanciful hope that she might be "the destined prophetess" of a new revelation, that of a sure ground for "mutual happiness" between man and woman. Here Hawthorne the myth-making creator and Hawthorne the Victorian commentator get entangled one with the other. Till the "Conclusion," the last few pages, Hester had remained, in ethics, a 'naturalist,' for whom 'sin,' in its Judaeo-Christian codification, had been a name or a convention. Now she is represented as comprehending that "no mission of divine and mysterious truth" can be entrusted to a woman "stained with sin, bowed down with shame, or even burdened with a life-long sorrow. The angel and apostle of the coming revelation must be a woman indeed, but lofty, pure, and beautiful, wise "through the ethereal medium of joy." Though this future "comprehension" is assigned to Hester, it is said in the voice of Hawthorne, the commentator, the husband of Sophia.

Whether applied to Hester specifically or to the mysterious new revelation to come—reminiscent of Anne Hutchinson, Mother Ann Lee, or Margaret Fuller, the pronouncement seems falsetto. Hawthorne's 'new revelation,' which seems (so far as I can understand it) not very new, is certainly not feminist but feminine and familial. Yet Hawthorne, I think, would allow Jesus His temptations and His sufferings: it is woman who is not permitted to be a *mater dolorosa*, whose nature is damaged, not illuminated and enriched, by sorrow.

Hester's voluntary return to the bleak cottage and the life of good works is intelligible enough without Hawthorne's 'revelation'—perhaps even without postulating her final penitence—which must mean her rejection of a naturalistic ethics, her acceptance of some kind of religious belief. Ghosts haunt the places where they died; college alumni return to the campuses where they spent, they nostalgically believe, the 'happiest years of their lives'; we all have 'unfinished business' which memory connects with the 'old home,' the town, the house, the room where we were miserable or joyful or, in some combination, both. There was a time, and there was a place, where, for whatever reason—perhaps just youth—we experienced, lived, belonged (if only by our *not belonging*).

Pearl, freed (like an enchanted princess) from her bondage, has married into some noble, or titled, European (not

British) family and is now a mother; but Hester is not the grandmotherly type, nor to be fulfilled in the role of dowager, knowing, as she does, that—whatever the state of Continental ignorance or sophisticated indulgence—her pearls are paste, her jewels, tarnished. There can be no autumnal worldly happiness for her. Without Christian faith, she must work out, work off, her Karma—achieve her release from selfhood.

IV

Hester's conceptions were altered by her experience; Dimmesdale's were not. Unlike her—and (in different and more professional fashion) the nineteenth-century agnostics Clough, Arnold, Leslie Stephen, and George Eliot—Dimmesdale was never seriously troubled by doubts concerning the dogmas of Christianity, as he understood them, and the ecclesiastical institution, the church, as he understood it. He was by temperament a "true priest": a man "with the reverential sentiment largely developed." Indeed, "In no state of society would he have been called a man of liberal views; it would always have been essential to his peace to feel the pressure of a faith about him, supporting, while it confined him within its iron framework."

Some aspects of Dimmesdale's rituals would seem to have been suggested by those of Cotton Mather, whom Barrett Wendell, in his discerning study, aptly called the "Puritan Priest." Though Mather's Diary was not published in full till 1911, striking extracts from it appeared as early as 1836 in W. B. C. Peabody's memoir, likely to have been read by Hawthorne. Dimmesdale's library was "rich with parchment-bound folios of the Fathers and the lore of the Rabbis and monkish erudition . . ."; and Mather (possessor of the largest private library in New England) was, as Hawthorne could see from the *Magnalia*, deeply versed in the Fathers and the Rabbis. Those aptitudes were, among the Puritan clergy, singular only in degree. But the "fastings and vigils" of Dimmesdale were, so far as I know, paralleled only by Mather's.

To fasts and vigils Dimmesdale added flagellations, unneeded by the thrice-married Mather. Dimmesdale's sin, one of *passion* and not of *principle* or even of *purpose*—these three possible categories are Hawthorne's—had been an act committed with horrible pleasurable surprise, after which (since the sin had been of passion) the clergyman had "watched with morbid zeal and minuteness . . . each breath of emotion, and his every thought."

It is by his capacity for passion—on the assumption that passionateness is a generic human category, and hence the man capable of one passion is capable of others—that Chillingworth first feels certain that he has detected Hester's lover. Having sketched a psychosomatic theory that bodily diseases may be "but a symptom of some ailment in the spiritual part," the "leech" declares that his patient is, of all men he has known, the one in whom body and spirit are the "closest conjoined"; Dimmesdale turns his eyes, "full and bright, and with a kind of fierceness," on the 'leech,' and then, with a "frantic gesture," rushes out of the room. Chillingworth comments on the betraying passion: "As with one passion, so with another! He hath done a wild thing erenow, this pious Master Dimmesdale, in the hot passion of his heart!"

If a common denominator between a burst of anger and a fit of lust is not immediately apparent, some sharedness there is: in both instances, reason and that persistence we call the self are made temporarily passive. A man's passions are—by contextual definition at least—*uncontrollable;* they 'get the better of' the habitual self. The man 'lets himself go'; is 'beside himself.' It is in this breakdown of habitual control that Chillingworth finds corroboration of what he suspected.

He finds more positive verification when he takes advantage of Dimmesdale's noonday nap to examine his "bosom," there finding, or thinking he finds, the *stigma* of the scarlet letter branded on the priestly flesh. In view of Hawthorne's emphasis—or, more strictly, Chillingworth's—on the close connection between soul and body in Dimmesdale, this *stigma* appears to be like (even though in reverse) the *stigmata* of Christ's wounds which some Catholic mystics are said to have manifested.

Hawthorne turns now to other aspects of Dimmesdale's

'case.' Consciousness of concealed sin may, like physical deformities, make one feel that everyone is watching him. And inability to give public confession to one's sin, the fact that (through cowardice or whatever) one cannot trust his secret to anyone, may make one equally suspicious of everyone—thus deranging one's proper reliance on some gradated series of trusts and confidences.

"Have a real reserve with almost everybody and have a seeming reserve with almost nobody; for it is very disagreeable to seem reserved, and very dangerous not to be so" is counsel bitter, but not unsage, of Lord Chesterfield. Dimmesdale has a real reserve with everyone and a seeming one, too, save when his passion briefly breaks down his habitual caution. But his cautious guard, his ever vigilant consciousness of what he conceals, has made him incapable of distinguishing between friend and foe, has broken down any confidence in what he might otherwise properly have relied upon, his intuitions. Dimly perceiving that some evil influence is in range of him, and feeling doubt, fear, sometimes horror and hatred at the sight of the old leech, he yet, knowing no rational reason for such feelings, distrusts the warnings of his deep antipathy.

Doubtless what most engaged Hawthorne's creative concern for Dimmesdale was the feature of ambivalence in his situation. Dimmesdale's sin and suffering had, in their way, educated the pastor and the preacher. Without his sin of passion and his sin of concealment, Dimmesdale would have been a man learned in books and theological abstractions but ignorant of 'life,' naive, unself-knowing. It was the self-education forced upon him by his sin which made him the pastor, the 'confessor,' the powerful preacher he is plausibly represented as becoming.

At the end of his seven years, Dimmesdale is a great—or as the American vulgate would have it, "an eminently successful" —pastor and preacher. By way of comparison, Hawthorne characterizes the categories into which his fellow-clergymen could be put—all types illustrated by Mather in the 'saints' lives' of the *Magnalia*. Some were greater scholars; some were "of a sturdier texture of mind than his, and endowed with a far greater share of shrewd, hard, iron, or granite understanding" (the preceding epithets show the noun to be used in the Coleridgean, or disparaging, sense); others, really saintly, lacked the Pentecostal gift of speaking "the heart's native language," of expressing "the highest truths through the medium of familiar words and images."

To the last of these categories Dimmesdale might, save for his "crime of anguish," have belonged. This burden kept him "on a level with the lowest," gave him his sympathy with the sinful—and his sad eloquence, sometimes terrifying, but oftenest persuasive and tender. These sermons made him loved and venerated; but their preacher knew well what made them powerful, and he was confronted with the old dilemma of means and ends.

In the pulpits Dimmesdale repeatedly intends to make a confession, and repeatedly he does; but it is a vague, a ritual confession—like that of the General Confession at Anglican Matins, except that the "miserable sinner" in whom there is no health is violently intensified by a consistently Calvinist doctrine of total depravity. No difference: Calvinist and Wesleyan and revivalist accusations against the total self can, with equal ease, become ritual. Dimmesdale never confesses to adultery or any other specific sin—only to total depravity: "subtle, but remorseful hypocrite," he knows how the congregation will take his rhetorical self-flagellation: as but the greater evidence of his sanctity; for the more saintly a man, the more conscious he is of even the most venial sins.

So the clergyman was fixed in his plight. At home, in his study, he practiced not only his physical act of penance, his self-scourging; but he practiced also a "constant introspection" which tortured without purifying. To what profit this penance unpreceded by penitence, this torturing introspection which led to no resolution, no action?

As he later told Lowell, Hawthorne had thought of having Dimmesdale confess to a Catholic priest (presumably some wandering French Jesuit) as he did, indeed, have Hilda confess to a priest in St. Peter's, not her sin (for she was 'sinless') but her complicity by witness to a sin and a crime. Such an idea might have crossed the mind of a Protestant "priest" of Dimmesdale's monkish erudition and practices. But, had he acted upon the impulse, and had the Jesuit been willing to hear the confession, there could have been no absolution, either sacramental or moral. Quite apart from having to change his religion, Dimmesdale would have had to do real penance, make real amends, and, had public confession been enjoined, not of his general sinfulness but of his specific sin, confess to the committing of adultery, and of that deeper, more spiritual, sin in which he had persisted for years, that of concealing the truth.

What has kept Dimmesdale from confession? Hester has herself been partly at fault, has made a serious error in judgment. At the beginning of the novel, Dimmesdale, her pastor, has, publicly in his professional capacity, enjoined her to speak. His injunction that she name her child's father reads ironically when one reverts to it after the chronicle of the "seven years" which ensue. "Be not silent from any mistaken pity and tenderness for him; for, believe me, Hester, though he were to step down from a high place, and stand there beside thee, on thy pedestal of shame, yet better were it so, than to hide a guilty heart through life. What can the silence do for him, except it tempt him—yea, compel him, as it were—to add hypocrisy to sin? . . . . Take heed how thou deniest to him— who, perchance, hath not the courage to grasp it for himself— the bitter, but wholesome, cup that is now presented to thy lips!"

Already Dimmesdale had, perhaps, begun to master the art he showed in his sermons—that of speaking the truth about himself to others (Hester excluded) in seeming to utter a salutary generalization. Arthur Dimmesdale is, "perchance," a coward, weak beside Hester, whose feeling toward him, never contemptuous, partakes certainly of the maternal. Would, she says, "that I might endure his agony as well as mine."

With all men, surely, the longer confession is delayed the

more difficult it becomes. The procrastination is 'rationalized' —even though the 'rationalization' never really satisfies the 'rationalizer.'

Dimmesdale, as we see him seven years after, appears to offer his basic rationalization in his speech to Chillingworth— expressed (like his injunction to Hester in the third chapter) in generalized, in hypothetical, terms: there are guilty men who, "retaining, nevertheless, a zeal for God's glory and man's welfare, . . . shrink from displaying themselves black and filthy in the view of men; because, thenceforward, no good can be achieved by them; no evil of the past be redeemed by better services."

There is some truth in what he says. And the Catholic Church, which consistently holds that the unworthiness of a priest does not invalidate the sacrament he administers, which conducts its confessionals not in the presence of a congregation, sees the degree of truth in Dimmesdale's position.

But, for all his Puritan priestliness, Dimmesdale is a Protestant; and the Catholic half-truth is not for him to appropriate. It is given to Chillingworth to utter the 'Protestant' truth. If men of secret sin "seek to glory God, let them not lift heavenward their unclean hands! If they would serve their fellow-men, let them do it by constraining them to penitential self-abasement!"

After her interview with her pastor on the midnight scaffold, Hester is shocked to reflect upon his state. "His nerve seemed absolutely destroyed. His moral force was abased into more than childish weakness." She reflects on her responsibility. Whether Hester's or Hawthorne's—two of her reflections appear to be intended as those of both, the commentator phrasing what Hester feels—the sentences read: "Here was the iron link of mutual crime, which neither he nor she could break. Like all other ties, it brought along with it its obligations." She must disclose to him Chillingworth's identity; must shield her lover.

So Hester assumes her maternal responsibility to her pastor and lover. In "The Pastor and his Parishioner" the titular roles are ironically reversed. The two meet in the "dim wood," "each a ghost, and awe-stricken at the other ghost." One chill hand touches another almost as chill; yet the grasp of the chill and the chill took away the penultimate chill of isolation which had separated them from all mankind. Their conversation "went onward, not boldly, but step by step. . . ." They "needed something slight and casual to run before and throw open the doors of intercourse, so that their real thoughts might be led across the threshold."

Their first "real thoughts" to find expression are the mutual questions—"Hast thou found peace?" Neither has. Hester tries to reassure Dimmesdale by taking the line, the pragmatic line, which the pastor has already used, in rationalized self-defense, to Chillingworth. He is not comforted. "Of penance I have had enough. Of penitence there has been none!"

Hester sees him, whom she "still so passionately loves," as on the verge of madness. She sees her worse-than-error—originally disguised from her, as an impulse generous and protective—in not letting her lover know that his fellow lodger, physician, and torturer was her husband; she confesses it. Dimmesdale is at first violent against her for her long silence, violent with all that "violence of passion" which first gave Chillingworth the notion that the pastor had, despite his purity, inherited "a strong animal nature from his father or his mother." Then he relents: "I freely forgive you now. May God forgive us both!" But he goes on to extenuate this sin by comparison with Chillingworth's: "We are not, Hester, the worst sinners in the world. There is one worse than even the polluted priest! That old man's revenge has been blacker than my sin. He has violated in cold blood the sanctity of a human heart. Thou and I, Hester, never did so!"

Then follow the famous words of Hester. The lovers, like Dante's yet more illustrious couple, had acted in hot blood, not in cold. And—"What we did had a consecration of its own. We felt it so! We said so to each other! Hast thou forgotten it?"

Dimmesdale replies, "Hush, Hester!. . . No; I have not

forgotten!" That Hester had said so is credible. It is difficult to credit the 'priest's' ever having used, even in the heat of romance, any such sacred word as "consecration," though Hester remembers the word as used by both; but Dimmesdale, though his "Hush" presumably implies that he in some way now thinks it wrong, does not contradict her recollection.

Then he appeals to Hester to rid him of Chillingworth and what Hester calls the "evil eye": "Think for me, Hester! Thou art strong. Resolve for me!" "Advise me what to do." And Hester accepts the responsibility. She fixes "her deep eyes" on her lover, "instinctively exercising a magnetic power" over his spirit, now "so shattered and subdued. . . ."

Dismissing Dimmesdale's talk about the Judgment of God, Hester immediately—like a sensible nineteenth-century physician or practical nurse—recommends a change of scene, an escape from an oppressive situation, and begins to outline alternatives. At first she speaks as though her lover (or former lover —one does not know which to call him) might escape alone: into the Forest to become, like the Apostle Eliot, his recent host, a preacher to the Redmen; or across the sea—to England, Germany, France, or Italy. How, exactly, a Calvinist clergyman, is to earn his living in Catholic France and Italy is not clear; but Hester seems to have unbounded faith in her lover's intellectual abilities and personal power, once he has shrugged off New England; she seems to think of his creed—and even of his profession—as historical accidents. These Calvinists, these "iron men, and their opinions" seem to her emancipated mind to have kept Arthur's "better part in bondage too long already!" He is to change his name, and, once in Europe, become "a scholar and a sage among the wisest and the most renowned of the cultivated world." He is bidden, "Preach! Write! Act! Do anything save to lie down and die!"

In all this appeal, Hester seems to project her own energy into Dimmesdale and, what is more, seems to show little understanding of her lover's nature: could he, eight years ago, have been a man to whom changing your name, your creed, your profession could have been thus lightly considered? Can

Dimmesdale ever have been a man of action in the more or less opportunist sense of which Hester sees him capable? If so, as an Oxford man (Hawthorne should have made him, as a Puritan, a Cantabrigian), he could have submitted to Archbishop Laud instead of coming to New England. What positive action do we know him to have committed in 'cold blood'? He committed a sin in hot blood once—it is tempting to say 'once,' and I have sometimes thought (unfairly perhaps) that Hester may have been the seducer. Otherwise his sins have been negative and passive—cowardice and hypocrisy.

False in its reading of his character and rashly oversanguine of programs as Hester's exhortation may be, Dimmesdale is temporarily aroused by her strength, by her belief that a man can forget his past, dismiss its 'mistakes' and 'debts,' and start again as though nothing had happened, as though he had neither memory nor conscience. For a moment indeed he believes he can start all over again, if only, invalid that he is, he has not to start alone. But Hester tells him that he will not go alone: her boldness speaks out "what he vaguely hinted at but dared not speak."

Hester and Arthur part, but not before she has made plans for passage on a vessel about to sail for Bristol. When the minister learns that it will probably be on the fourth day from the present, he notes but to himself, not to Hester, on the fortunate timing.

It is "fortunate" because three days hence Dimmesdale is to preach the Election Sermon, the highest civic honor a Bay Colony clergyman could receive. That Dimmesdale should still be pleased, should still look to this ending of his career as a dramatic close, that he should still think of his public duty more than of his private morality shocks Hawthorne as, of all Dimmesdale's doings and not-doings the most "pitably weak." What is it, finally, but professional vanity? "No man, for any considerable period can wear one face to himself, and another to the multitude, without finally getting bewildered as to which may be the true."

The minister walks home from the Forest "in a maze,"

confused, amazed. Hester's bold suggestions have temporarily released him from that iron framework which both confines and supports him. His habitual distinctions between right and wrong have broken down; and all that survives is his sense of decorum.

"At every step he was incited to do some strange, wild, wicked thing or other, with a sense that it would be at once involuntary and intentional; in spite of himself, yet growing out of a profounder self than that which opposed the impulse" —'profounder' in a sense Hawthorne does not define. It may be a man's subconscious or his "total depravity" left to himself— the Dark Forest in man, the Satanic.

All of his impulses are rebellions against his habitual mode of life and even, one would say, of thought and feeling. Meeting with one of his elderly deacons, he has the impulse to utter "certain blasphemous suggestions that rose in his mind respecting the communion supper." And, encountering the oldest woman of his church, pious and deaf and mostly concerned with recollecting her 'dear departed,' he can think of no comforting text from Scripture but only what then seemed to him an "unanswerable argument against the immortality of the soul" which, happily, she is too deaf to hear. To a pious young girl, he is tempted to give "a wicked look" and say one evil word, and averts the temptation only by rudeness; and to some children, just begun to talk, he wants to teach "some very wicked words." Lastly, meeting a drunken seaman from the ship upon which he plans to sail, he longs to share with the abandoned wretch the pleasure of "a few improper jests" and a volley of good round oaths; and it is not his virtue but his "natural good taste" and still more his "habit of clerical decorum" which dissuade him.

These temptations exhibit a Dimmesdale I should not have guessed to exist even in unvoiced capacity—and for which Hawthorne has given no preparation: indeed, we are never given any account of the pastor's English prehistory at all comparable to that which is furnished for Hester. "The Minister in a Maze" is, indeed, something of a brilliant sketch, a 'set piece'—

something which occurred to Hawthorne as he was writing his novel, yet does not wholly fit it. Can the pastor once have been a young rake?

It is unlikely. To be sure, some of the Puritans, including the Puritan clergy, were converted not only from their ancestral Anglicanism but from worldliness if not anything more precisely sinful. And at Oxford and elsewhere Dimmesdale may have heard oaths and smutty stories, even though his principles and taste have forbidden him to use them. Likely Hawthorne meant us to see in this amazing scene a brief resurgence of that inherited "strong animal nature" which had for a lifetime, but for a lapse of act and another of feeling, been so rigorously repressed.

This brilliant chapter, if defended, will have to be defended on psychological considerations more general than specifically relevant to Hawthorne's clergyman. In the benign phenomenon called 'conversion'—the selves of a divided self reorder themselves: the self which was dominant is exorcised, or at any event decisively subordinated; the self which existed as subordinate—the 'good self'—becomes supreme, or nearly supreme. And there is a corresponding shift of positions which we may call perversion. Both of these changes with certain types of men, can occur—or show themselves—suddenly, in a moment. Some of these reorganizations persist; some are brief, impelled as they oftenest appear to be, by the 'magnetism' of an emotionally powerful propagandist—such an one as Hester.

In yielding to Hester's proposals of escape, Dimmesdale, says Hawthorne, had, in effect, made such a bargain with Satan as the witch-lady, Mistress Hibbins, suspected him of. "Tempted by a dream of happiness, he had yielded himself with deliberate choice, as he had never done before, to what he knew was deadly sin." This he now has done. Hester, out of one generous impulse, spared identifying Chillingworth to her lover and *concealed* her lover's name from Chillingworth, and now out of another 'generous' impulse she had bade her lover to escape his concealed sin not by revealing it but by abandoning his adopted country, his profession, even his name. And what have been the results of these 'generous' impulses—not wholly disinterested, perhaps, since she thinks of being re-united to her lover? What have been the results of these attempts modern Americans understand so well—attempts to help, by sparing, those we love, or think we love?

Dimmesdale returns to his study, conscious that his old self has gone. The man who returned from the Forest is wiser —wiser about himself, than the man who entered it. But—like Donatello's—what a "bitter kind of knowledge." He throws the already written pages of his sermon into the fire, and, after having eaten "ravenously," works all night on another.

What, the attentive reader speculates, is the difference be-tween the unfinished sermon written before the Forest and the finished one of the night that followed? That difference, like the nature of the sermon delivered, seems curiously irrelevant to Hawthorne. We are told that the new discourse was written "with such an impulsive flow of thought and emotion" that its writer "fancied himself inspired." Which is the word to be stressed: *fancied* or *inspired?* We are told that he wrote with "earnest haste and ecstasy": which of the three words are we to stress? Had he something to say in the sermon which was the result of his intention (premeditated at some time before he delivered the sermon) or there after taking his stand beside Hester on the scaffold? Did the sermon have some new tone in it, some tragic or bitter wisdom wrested from that gross lapse into illusion which so bemused and amazed him as he returned from the Forest?

Melville once wrote a masterly and prophetic sermon for Father Mapple. Hawthorne writes none for Dimmesdale. Dur-ing the delivery of the sermon, we readers, with Hester, are outside the meeting house. We but hear the preacher's voice, are told of its great range of pitch, power, and mood. Yet, says Hawthorne, if an auditor listened "intently, and for the pur-pose," he would always have heard throughout the "cry of pain," the cry of a human heart "telling its secret, whether of guilt or sorrow. . . ." Yet in this respect, surely, the present sermon was not unique; for it had always been "this profound and continual undercurrent that gave the clergyman his most appropriate power."

When, after the sermon, we learn dimly from the admiring congregation its burden, we discover, strange to say, that it had ended with a prophetic strain. It had not been a Jeremiad—a denunciation of the Chosen people, but a foresight of New England's "high and glorious destiny." This is puzzling to interpret. That the preacher, about to declare himself an avowed sinner, cannot (like Cotton Mather) denounce his New England's sins, I can see; but why need he celebrate its high destiny? Is it that Hawthorne, to whom the 'subject matter' of the sermon does not seem to matter, has inserted and asserted, his own strong regional loyalties?

What ought to matter to the constructor of so closely constructed a novel seems not to have mattered to Hawthorne. What matters to him, and evokes his harsh rebuke, is that, seeing the error of escape, Dimmesdale has planned first to give the sermon, thus triumphantly ending his professional career, and then to make his public confession. The giving of the sermon as such, and the content of the sermon, do not really concern him—unless the giving of the sermon contributes the publicity and the drama of the scaffold confession requisite to counterpart the publicity and the drama of that first scaffold on which Hester stood—save for her baby on her arm—alone.

Implied is some final clash of wills and 'philosophies' between Hester and Arthur. Dimmesdale bids Pearl and Hester toward the scaffold. Pearl, birdlike, flies and puts her arms around his knees; but Hester comes slowly, "as if impelled by fate and against her strongest will," and pauses before she reaches him. Only when Chillingworth attempts to stop the pastor's public confession and the pastor again appeals does Hester come. But Dimmesdale has assumed the man's role at last—or a man's role: he asks Hester for her physical strength to help him onto the scaffold, but in asking her strength enjoins, "let it be guided by the will which God hath granted me." When they stand together, he murmurs to Hester, "Is not this better than what we dreamed of in the Forest?" Hester cannot assent.

She palliates with "I know not"; then adds what seems to mean 'better, perhaps, if we two and little Pearl can die together.' But that, though human, is melodramatic. Hester must see that her lover is dying and that there is no way save a supernatural intervention—an 'act of God,' as insurance companies put it—which can kill her and the child concurrently with him.

After his confession to his parish and the revelation of his *stigma*, he says farewell to Hester. She speaks of their having "ransomed one another" by their consequent miseries, speaks of spending their "immortal life" together. He replies, as he did to her words in the Forest about the private "consecration" of their adulterous union. "Hush, Hester. . . . The law we broke!—the sin here so awfully revealed.—let these alone be in thy thoughts! I fear! I fear!" What he fears is not for his own salvation—assured, to his perception, apparently, by this, his deathbed repentance and confession—but for any reunion of the lovers after death.

v

It seems, to so close a reading as I have given to Dimmesdale, a pity that Hawthorne's "deeper psychology," and his own commentary, stop at this point. What is one to think of deathbed repentances, and of repentance so dramatic as this? And was not the repentance, if repentance there was and not yet another form of proud illusion, finally produced not by Chillingworth's malign sleuthing but by Hester's 'generous' and—in view of her lover's theology and character, if not indeed judged by any kind of absolute ethic—immoral advice that he escape from the consequences of his deed?

These are questions partly casuistical, partly universal, all of which one would expect to have interested Hawthorne. That they are not 'worked' out is partly, perhaps, Hawthorne's judgment that from earlier comments might be inferred the comments here relevant; partly, I think, a felt conflict between aesthetic and ethico-psychological considerations: aesthetically, he wants a firm, dramatic finale—something at all times difficult for him to manage, and here one which must be reconciled as best he can with his ethically psychological concerns, his probings and questionings.

Lastly, his 'conclusion' must give the modes of interpretation which the community apply to the phenomenon of the *stigma* which "most," though not all, of the spectators testified to having seen when the dying 'priest' bared his breast. In *The Scarlet Letter*, even more than in his later romances, Hawthorne sees life from inside the consciousness of a few persons—those of an introspective and meditative turn; but these persons, however insulated, are not solipsists: they believe, as Hawthorne believes, in a world they have not created by their own consciousness but merely interpreted.

The community forms, in terms of literary tradition, a Greek chorus, to the happenings in his protagonists' inner lives. Like the utterances in the choruses of Sophocles, it doesn't provide what a novice enamored of classical antiquity expects— the voice of true wisdom, the sure guide by which to interpret the too intense, and hence probably aberrative, views of the protagonists. When such a novice reads Arnold's famous praise of Sophocles that he "saw life steadily and saw it whole," the novice looks to the chorus to give that steady and whole interpretation. But the expectation is vain: the chorus partly comments, half empathetically, on what goes forward at the center of the stage, partly utters traditional maxims and apothegms.

In Hawthorne's choruses the same is true. In *The Scarlet Letter*, there are many auctorial comments on the community —comments frequently not limited to that seventeenth-century Puritan community in which Arthur and Hester lived. It is impossible to reduce them to any unitary and propositional form. Hawthorne is no Utopian, whether of the Brook Farm or any other variety; he is equally free from any extravagant individualism, even of the Emersonian variety: I say 'Emersonian' because Emerson himself was no such individualist as the half-gifted, half-eccentric people who appealed to his ears and sheltered themselves under his name.

Hawthorne's 'community'—or 'society'—is now kind, now persecuting; now foolish, now wise. Perhaps his most characteristic view of it is that, given time enough, 'the people' will show wisdom and do justice. *Given time enough*, it will forget initial suspicions and hostilities—do justice to the relatively heretic individualists—Edwards, Emerson, Thoreau, Garrison, Anne Hutchinson. What if it has not time?

The relation between individual truth (that of existential insight) and the community's slowly shifting 'wisdom' can never be either perfectly or permanently adjusted. Seneca wrote, "As often as I have been among men, I returned home less a man than I was before." But Aristotle opens his *Politics* with the maxim that "A man who can live alone must be either a god or a beast." *Society and Solitude* (the title of Emerson's last collection of essays) names two resorts, the two forces which must ever be 'checking' and 'balancing' each other.

Hawthorne's 'absolute truth' and 'ultimate reality' are not to be identified with any of their adumbrations. They are not imparted in their wholeness to Dimmesdale, or Hester, or to the chorus of the community, nor to Hawthorne as commentator on his own myth, nor to the author of this essay. We all know but in part, and prophesy but in part. Generalizations without case histories are commonplaces; case histories without the attempt at formulating 'first principles' are but (in the pejorative sense) casuistries.

This dialectical nature of truth-finding and truth-reporting Hawthorne was too honest to evade; it is to his literary as well as his 'philosophical' credit.

1965

Emily Dickinson

Emily Dickinson was a person, a local personage, something of a local myth all the while she was writing her private poems. Now she remains a personality; she has become a literary type and myth as well. In 1890, when the slim gray volume of her *Poems* appeared, perceptive readers recognized their merit and made out their approximate physiognomy without more knowledge of the author's life than the scant facts given by Colonel Higginson in his Preface. And, had she not continued to be read, as a poet, there would be no desire for further knowledge of her life. But then, in the 1920's, as she continued to be read, an ambitious literary niece produced mysteries and aroused curiosity. Other literary women sought to solve puzzles she had, in part, created—to identify the lover, renouncing whom, Emily became something like a metaphysical poet of love.

That period, it is to be hoped, has come to an end. Yet the eager work of detection has had its use. The names of candidates for the honor may be recorded and remembered for the sake of giving a texture of specificity, as well as to suggest how little a single identification matters. But what emerges, and remains for the reader of poetry, is the type of experience behind the poetry, the mythic type of the poet—the New England spinster, intense, responding to slight pressures, who can find a world in a room.

In her regionally informed, most sensible and sensitive biography, Mrs. Millicent Todd Bingham, the daughter of Emily's first editor, takes in her stride Emily's loves, real or imaginary; and she cites the testimony of Emily's brother, William Austin. A year his sister's senior, Austin was a collector of paintings and enamored of shrubs, the honorable assumptor of his father's responsibilities to college, town, and family, yet a more flexible and troubled character. Austin, the affectionate brother, to whom, while a youth away from Amherst, Emily wrote copious letters, who, as a married man, lived next door, seems a competent judge of his sister's personality. It is his testimony that "at different times" Emily "had been devoted to several men." He even went so far as to maintain that she had been several times in love, in her own way. But he denied that because of her devotion to any one man she forsook all others. Emily "reached out eagerly, fervently even, toward anybody who lighted the spark. . . ."

Whether or not she was "several times in love," she certainly had many loves. There was a succession of males to whom she attached her devotion: some of them, like Gould, Humphrey, Newton, and Colonel Higginson, her "teachers"; some, more awesome characters—fathers.

The Reverend Dr. Charles Wadsworth certainly mattered to Emily; and the time of his removal from Philadelphia to San Francisco, a distance prohibitive of prompt access to him by letter, coincides with significant alterations in her life and poetry. Yet this was a fantasy of love, constructed about a man whom she scarcely knew and who was doubtless never aware of her idealization; and her sense for the real always won out over whatever presented attractive fantasy.

Edward Dickinson was a version of God the Father: stern, implacable, yet a tower and rock of strength; mysterious in his ways, but doubtless always acting for the best, a man of moral rigidity who was none the less capable of ringing the church bell as for a fire so that his neighbors would emerge from their houses to share an Aurora Borealis. Her feeling for her father was, probably, dominant. Her "poems about God," the "Papa in Heaven," are little girl compounds of pertness and humility addressed to a powerful and puzzling big man, to Admirable Omnipotence. Her figures psychically distant and impressive—Father, the Reverend Dr. Wadsworth, Mr. Bowles, the editor of the Springfield *Republican*, Judge Otis Lord—were all 'Fathers'; and God she made in their image and likeness.

God was her archetypal Lover. The God whom she reverenced was not the Son, the "Paragon of Chivalry," like her brother Austin, but God the Father—the Lover at once infinitely attractive and infinitely awesome, one partly revealed by the Son and His nature, but only partly revealed; finally, the unattainable God. "He who loves God cannot strive that God should love him in return." This injunction comes from Spinoza; but the spirit of it appears also as the deepest tone of the New England Theology.

All of Emily's loves were unattainable: either members of her family or women or married men; and they were doubtless loved, in her way, precisely because they were unattainable—did not, could not, expose, even to herself, the nature of her dedication.

Emily's life is no riddle. New England has had many maiden ladies like her, and many widows who are like maiden ladies. There are many who have loved unsuccessfully or insuitably—whom fear or pride have kept from the married state; many who have loved 'above them,' could love in no other way, and who prefer singleness to some equalizing union. The father who prefers his daughters not to marry, who needs them at home with him, is matched by the daughter so filial as to prefer the familiar order. There is nothing monstrous—or even necessarily thwarted or blighted—about such women. They have their friends and their duties; they can nurture their own sensibilities and spiritualities—sharpen in consciousness.

Many gradually withdraw from the world, as Emily did. The circumference shrinks as friends die or depart; the pattern of life becomes more rigid. But the withdrawal can be gain if there is something to withdraw to. Many spinsters have, like Emily, their brand of humor, their mode of ritual—perhaps even their habitual way of dressing; but what differentiates

Emily is that she had her poetry. She need not avert or circumvent woe save by the stratagem of poetry. She need not keep her grief to herself; she could give it to consciousness and to paper—could face it by naming it.

Richnesses sustained Emily—among them her sense of 'degree,' of status, of family. Of 'degree' she was positively and negatively aware. When she wasn't a little girl, to be fed a crumb, she was a Queen or an Empress, jeweled and triumphant on a throne. At once no man was 'good enough' for her to marry, and those higher than she were so much higher as to seem out of reach or else, in fantasy, grandly, by their election, to lift her to equality.

She was a Dickinson, the daughter of a 'Squire,' whose father had been one of the founders of Amherst College, whose brother was, if epigone, the honorable successor to greatness. The bonds between her and her family were such as to sustain her pride.

She was not, however she might seem to Boston, a rural poetess or spinster, but a princess. When Colonel Higginson proposed visits to Boston, access to her intellectual and literary 'peers' (Julia Ward Howe, for example, or Mrs. Sargent with her monthly convenings of paper readers and polite disputants), Emily could not be moved from Amherst. She never came to Higginson: he, and other professed admirers, had to go to her, to her home, where she could set the tone and dictate the ritual. Emerson might leave Concord for the Saturday Club; like Thoreau, Emily stayed at home.

It has often been regretted that she did not, like Whitman, tender her poems to Emerson's sympathetic inspection rather than to Higginson's mixture of sympathy and deprecation; but Emerson, despite his elegant courtesy, his mode of listening to others, could not at once be heeded—and dismissed. Emerson was polished "granite"—a master, like Emily herself, and (unlike her chosen mentor) a master in a domain too closely impinging on her own. In reputation above her, she was a poet-in-verse of a kind he but adumbrated.

How perceptive, how shrewd to estimate who and what

could serve her was this New England spinster. She seized upon what she needed, and this possession sufficed: she had no taste for superfluities.

I I

Among New Englanders, Emily stands (as Allen Tate has long ago remarked) between Emerson and Hawthorne—of whom she wrote that he "entices—appalls." Her rearing was in Trinitarian Congregationalism—often in New England villages referred to as, in distinction from the Unitarian heresy, the "Orthodox" Church. Unlike the rest of her family (some of whom capitulated early, some late), Emily never 'joined the church,' never would fix the content of her belief. But she knew what her neighbors and her pastor believed, and (like Emerson in his attack on Harvard College) had the personal comfort and poetic license of cherishing favorite skepticisms without supposing that they would undermine, and hence render impossible of satire and attack, the solid faith of others, the solid force of institutions. She lacks Hawthorne's sense of sin; and isolation for privacy is hardly an evil to her; the analogy to Hawthorne lies rather in her obsession with death and futurity, still more in the sense of mystery: as in the remark (put upon the lips of Holgrave), "I begin to suspect that a man's bewilderment is the measure of his wisdom." Her deepest poems are metaphysical or tragic; her mode of vision symbolist; her thinking, analogical. Emerson (whose *Essays* an early "tutor" gave her) probably flexed her mind, encouraged her speculations and her questionings of orthodoxy; but her mythology remains—what Hawthorne's was, and Emerson's never—Biblical and Trinitarian. Though a rebel, she is not, like Emerson, a schismatic.

A third ancestor comes often to mind—Sir Thomas Browne, a writer cherished by the nineteenth-century New Englanders, especially by the Concord men, and known and cited by Emily. "For prose," she wrote Colonel Higginson, she had "Mr. Ruskin, Sir Thomas Browne, and the *Revelations*." These are very special kinds of prose certainly; and Emily's poetic style is not only that of some Emerson poems ("The

74

Humble Bee," "Hamatreya." "Mithridates," "Days") but that of Browne's *Religio* and *Christian Morals*. Her world view is the Brunonian sense of the natural world, so full of curious objects in the eyes of most men—though, as Browne remarks, he doesn't know how we call the toad ugly when it was made by the express design of God to assume that shape. Nor is Emily going to simplify the complexity of a God who made the bat. Of the bat, she writes:

> *Deputed from what Firmament—*
> *Of what Astute Abode—*
> *Empowered with what Malignity*
> *Auspiciously withheld—*
>
> *To his adroit Creator*
> *Ascribe no less the praise—*
> *Beneficent, believe me,*
> *His Eccentricities—*

Browne heaps up technical difficulties which beset the acceptance of the Bible and orthodox theology: he delights to list such difficulties as occasioned Bishop Colenso (pilloried by Arnold) the loss of his faith—the statistics of an Ark capable of holding all the creatures said to have entered.

Emily's most characteristic difficulties are with the morals of the Bible, especially of the Old Testament—which in her time and place had not been subjected to the 'Higher Criticism.' She 'knew her Bible' well, the total Bible: it was her prime mythology. She neither rejects it, nor accepts it without question and reservation. Its histories are rich and plausible human documents; its doctrinal books, like St. Paul's epistles, are testimonials apt for consideration; propose questions and speculations for her theological sensibility to ponder. She would have been shocked equally by having the Bible accepted as an infallible silencer of speculation or by having it treated as negligible, or even as 'literature.'

Her famous "The Bible is an antique Volume" was, to be sure, originally written for her nephew Ned and given the title, "Diagnosis of the Bible, by a Boy"; but the boy was not alien to the woman who understood his boredom and his bafflement: the final version is hers.

> *The Bible is an antique Volume—*
> *Written by faded Men*
> *At the suggestion of Holy Spectres—*
> *Subjects—Bethlehem*
> *Eden—the ancient Homestead—*
> *Satan—the Brigadier—*
> *Judas—the Great Defaulter—*
> *David—the Troubadour—*
> *Sin—a distinguished Precipice*
> *Others must resist—*
> *Boys that "believe" are very lonesome—*
> *Other Boys are "lost"—*
> *Had but the Tale a warbling Teller—*
> *All the Boys would come—*
> *Orpheus' Sermon captivated—*
> *It did not condemn—*

The sympathy with Satan and Judas is for rebels against laws they don't understand, or it comes from a feeling that, since sin must needs come into the world, and since the Crucifixion was foretold and necessary, we should not be too merciless on the unhappy perpetrators. The mushroom is a "Judas Iscariot" to the rest of Nature. Elsewhere she remarks that there are shocking instances of God's injustice: "Moses wasn't fairly used; Ananias wasn't." But it's temerarious to make such protestations. The same God who made the Lamb made the Lion: He who provided good, and suffers the little ones to come unto Him, also permits sin and evil.

There have been times in which the pious felt the need to defend God, to prop Him up—as though it were our business to support the Rock and Word, and to comfort the Comforter. Emily is too orthodox, too inclusive, to forget that behind God the Son, Himself sturdy, is God the Father, the Creator of all things and the Abyss of Godhead, unexhausted by what

His creatures understand of His ways: moving in a mysterious way His wonders to perform, and best known not defining Him.

Yet, in allowing for God's ways not being our ways, we mustn't use language equivocally but apply, even if in vain, our humanly highest standards. Writing on Abraham, Isaac, and God, Emily doesn't hesitate to identify God with "tyranny" and to find the moral of the averted human sacrifice in the reflection that, even with a "Mastiff," "Manners may prevail." The Divine existence Emily never doubts. The "fop, the Carp, the Atheist" value the present moment, yet "their commuted feet/ The Torrents of Eternity/ Do all but inundate."

> *The abdication of Belief*
> *Makes the Behavior small—*
> *Better an ignis fatuus*
> *Than no illume at all—*

"Belief, it does not fit so well/When altered frequently." There must be a Heaven because there certainly are saints on earth; and sanctity argues its survival. But how to prove a sky to a mole? *"Too much proof affronts Belief."* The turtle won't try to demonstrate to us that he can move—but, when we have turned our backs, he has. "That oblique Belief which we call conjecture" is the attempt to guess what Heaven is like, to picture "What eye hath not seen," the look of the "mansions" of Heaven. Emily speculates on the state of the dead: whether they know what is happening to us or are too removed; or whether, on the contrary, they are nearer to us for the absence of their bodies. But these are conjectures unanswered by Scriptures. Straight belief is uncircumstantial; content to affirm what it cannot map or delineate. And, for Emily, belief is straight.

III

Some years ago, a young literary man worked out a chart of Emily Dickinson's poetic development, one which set off as 'early' her conventional and sentimental verses, and using as tests for successive maturements the increasing substitution of assonance and consonance for rhyme, the increasing boldness and precision. He postulated a consistency of method; expected the poems systematically to grow more Dickinsonian. Having achieved her manner, her own style, she could not, he supposed, have turned back to period styles or others not demonstrably her own.

The theory, worked out before any scientific dating of her poems had been established, or even attempted, was too neat—perhaps predictably too neat. In any case, it has been effectually disproved by the massive edition of her poetry which Thomas Johnson has published, arranging the poems in a chronological order based upon the best modern objective methods of dating.

Emily did, to the end, 'look back.' Unlike Hopkins and James (or Mozart and Beethoven), she had no 'late style' so integrally held that she could not, in conscience, deviate therefrom.

In 1860 Emily wrote "If I shouldn't be alive/When the Robins come" (with its admirable "trying/With my Granite lip") and "How many times these low feet staggered—Only the soldered mouth can tell." Yet in the same year she wrote the sentimental piece with its bit of Scots—probably represented for her by Burns—"Poor little Heart!/Did they forget thee?/Then dinna care!" and the balladic repetition of "That scalds me now—that scalds me now." In 1861 she wrote "There's a certain Slant of light," but she also wrote "Why—do they shut Me out of Heaven"—one of her "little girl" pieces.

In "about 1865" she wrote the admirable quatrain:

> *To help our Bleaker Parts*
> *Salubrious Hours are given*
> *Which if they do not fit for Earth*
> *Drill silently for Heaven—*

She had written "Arrange the Heart" and rejected it for "Drill silently"—an improvement both in sparing the "Heart" and in giving the double-sensed *drill* (the martial discipline; the carpenter's tool if not then the dentist's also). Yet in the same time she wrote "Let down the Bars, Oh Death," a tritely sentimental sheep-and-shepherd poem.

In short, Emily added to her styles without subtracting; and in maturity she wrote a new kind of poetry without relinquishing the liberty of slipping back into her earlier modes.

It used to be said of Emerson that his 'bad' rhymes were due to a deficient ear—a theory once and for all disproved by the publication, in the first volume of Rusk's edition of the *Letters*, of Emerson's earliest poems, written in perfectly accurate heroic couplets. Indeed, even young Whitman could rhyme and meter acceptably. And Emily's first known verses, written in the early 1850's, demonstrate likewise that her subsequent deviation was purposed. Her "Valentine" poem faithfully rhymes "swain" and "twain," "air" and "fair." Neither Emerson nor Emily would have become known as poets for these 'correct' productions. By intuition, and by relatively conscious theorizing, they had to create new kinds of poetry.

Like Whitman, Emily took off from Emerson, whose *Poems* and *Essays* she owned and knew. But Whitman took off from Emerson's theory of the poet and his rhetorical essays; Emily, from Emerson's own practices as a poet: his short-lined rhyming; his gnomic quatrains, and gnomic poems like "Brahma"; his "Hamatreya," with its rustic diction and purposed and expressive metrical irregularity.

This lineage from Emerson was blended with another lineage—that of the hymnal. Several times she quotes Isaac Watts's hymn beginning, "There is a land of pure delight":

> *Could we but climb where Moses stood*
> *And view the landscape o'er,*
> *Nor Jordan's stream, nor death's cold flood,*
> *Should fright us from the shore;*

and the stanza, with its alternating 4 and 5, remains one of her metrical favorites. She creates a counterpoint or descant on Watts, relaxing the rhyming of lines 1 and 3 and individualizing Watts's congregational or communal "we":

'Tis not the Dying hurts us so—
'Tis Living—hurts us more—
But Dying—is a different way—
A Kind behind the Door

Short meter, long meter, common meter (the standard hymn stanza) are her mold, not to break but to render pliant.

Emily's language is her own mixture of provincialisms, the standard speech of her time, the concrete and the abstract, the words of young people and the theological words of orthodox preachers—such words as "infinite." Her use of language is at its best both meditated and precise. Worksheet drafts for a few of her poems provide the lists of alternatives between which she chose. In the poem on the Bible, the epithet finally elected—"warbling"—was chosen out of these possible dissyllables: "typic, hearty, bonnie, breathless, spacious, tropic, warbling, ardent, friendly, magic, pungent, winning, mellow." None of these dissyllables seems inevitable; but "warbling"— the unpremeditated singing of a bird or a rustic—seems the best candidate. Of a clergyman ("He preached upon 'Breadth' till it argued him narrow") she asserts satirically that Jesus would not know how to "meet so *enabled* a Man," choosing her epithet from a list which included "learned, religious, accomplished, discerning, accoutred, established, conclusive." Emily needs a trisyllabic word: but she certainly also distinguished it from "able": to "enable" is legally, as by authority, to make one what, by nature, he is *not:* it suggests the pretentiousness of borrowed righteousness or of learning extraneous to the personality.

Previous editions have printed the last stanza of "I never saw a Moor" as:

I never spoke with God
Nor visited in heaven—
Yet certain am I of the spot
As if the chart were given.

Johnson's new edition gives, for the conventional "chart," the word "checks," in the colloquial sense of railroad tickets—

quoting in adequate support Emily's prose, "My assurance of existence of Heaven is as great as though, having surrendered my checks to the conductor, I knew that I had arrived there." Madame Bianchi printed, in *Unpublished Poems*, one beginning, "A Visitor in March"; Johnson, a better reader of her aunt's difficult hand, alters "March" to "Marl." The "Visitor Is Death"; and the word "marl" means an earthy, crumbling deposit chiefly of clay, mixed with calcium carbonate, or earth (in the sense of clay): it means the cadaver. These two examples will illustrate that Emily used the words she meant and the gain of their restoration.

IV

Superficially, Emily is in the line of those village versifiers whose function was to elegize the dead in broadside or for incision on slate or marble gravestones; and many of her poems were either composed or later made to serve as tributes to her deceased relatives, friends, Amherst acquaintances, the distant admired (Charlotte Brontë and George Eliot). Then, too, she was reared in a period in which poets like Poe and Bryant (who celebrated death from youth into age), anthologies like Cheever's *Poets of America*, and newspaper elegies made the topic appear particularly suited to verse. The frequency with which deaths and accidents appeared in her newspaper, the Springfield *Republican*, prompted Emily to ask a friend in 1853: "Who writes those funny accidents, where railroads meet each other unexpectedly, and gentlemen in factories get their heads cut off quite informally?" It was Amherst custom, as it was elsewhere in New England, to visit cemeteries on Sunday afternoons. The local graveyard adjoined the Dickinson orchard on Pleasant Street; funeral processions passed by the Dickinson house.

These circumstances offer a regional tradition and mollify, if not remove, suspicion of Emily's morbidity. But, if they extenuate, they do not explain Emily's death poems, which are unlike Poe's and unlike Bryant's.

To the most cursory scanner, Emily was much obsessed

by death, 'Goings away,' departures, whether to geographic distances or by felt disloyalties. Spatial and psychic separations, absences, all disjunctions, can be felt, and were, by Emily, as deaths. In a rather usual pattern of reaction, she wrote her Death poems with a quality of magnitude almost proportioned to, for her, the unimportance of the intimated 'person in mind' —who served as occasion for a poem, not its motive or momentum.

Emily's "white election," it appears, began around the year 1862. This "white election": could it not have been Emily's acceptance of Death? What 'facts' can be supposed to explain the 'problem' of Emily point to some one, a person unacknowledgeable to her consciousness. Her poems suggest compelled flights from impending, threatening consciousness of that person or persons.

What anger we feel when one whom we had loved, or protested we did, 'dies on us.' He or she has up and left us. Ashamed of anger toward the 'loved dead'—or those loved who have separated from us, one denies the feeling. Emily's "white election" is not wholly devoid of moral blackmail, consequent guilts—rich pasture for poetry.

The poems about death are ranging in kind and tone. Emily's poems about death are sometimes written from the point of view of the observer; in others, she is witnessing her own death by anticipation ('You'll be sorry when I'm dead' or 'I want to die'); in others she is contemplating present destitution by the loss of others ("My life closed twice before its close"). The poems don't have to be in the first person to be self-regarding.

> On such a night, or such a night,
> Would anybody care
> If such a little figure
> Slipped quiet from its chair—

and " 'Twas the old—road—through pain" and the other poems about the death of a little girl seem, unavoidably, Emily in such postures, quite as much as "If I shouldn't be alive. . . ."

In reading the poems about death, one is temerarious in

distinguishing the observed from the imagined or fictive. "Looking at Death, is Dying" is an axiom to be attended—even though it occurs in a poem not about death but about loss.

The dead are variously conceived of—sometimes as in their graves, quiet despite the bustle of the day and of history. ("How many times these low feet staggered," "Safe in their Alabaster Chambers"). "I'm sorry for the Dead—Today," light in tone, lightly pities the sleeping farmers and their wives who "rest" while the festival of haying goes on in the village about them. In another poem, the grave is a cottage where a girl plays at "Keeping house" and prepares "marble tea." And the gravestone is a kind of death mask for the dead beneath it: it tries to thank those who gave the robin a "Memorial crumb," and tries with "Granite lip."

Perhaps the most brilliant of the death-in-death poems is "A Clock stopped—/Not the Mantel's," a masterpiece in the employment of a conceit coterminous with the poem—a definition once proposed for Donne's poems but more accurately applied to such of Emily's as this. Most of what is said fits approximately both sides of the equation; and that intellectual work which is the conceit serves, as we know, to distance the poem.

Like a train, a clock may be felt near to animate. In fable, a clock stops when its owner dies; at any event, it measures the clock time by which men live. The Doctor is a "Shopman," a clock repairer; but he cannot set the heart's pendulum swinging again. To the dead, hours and minutes and "Seconds" are alike now meaningless. They are meaningless compared with the "Decades" (more than the meter can justify this understatement for "centuries"), the "Decades of Arrogance" which separate "Dial life" from the "Degreeless Noon" of Eternity. The "Trinket," the diminutively precious object, has gained the accrual of "awe"; for the onlooker feels the "Arrogance" of the dead—their unconcern for us.

This poem appears to take the stance of the onlooker; but does it? It can well be argued that the poet imagines herself at the lofty distance of death, envisages how those others will feel as they watch and witness. In a poem like this the distinction between the imagined and the imaginer becomes impossible to fix. "There's a certain Slant of light" is a poem ostensibly about winter afternoons with their "Heavenly Hurt" and their "Seal, Despair"; when that winter light goes, " 'tis like the Distances/On the look of Death." In this poem "Death" is a metaphor for winter light, and at the same time winter light is a metaphor for death: one inclines to say, preponderantly the latter. "I like a look of Agony/Because I know it's true" invokes the glazing of the eyes in death; but "Beads upon the Forehead" are invoked by "Anguish"; and the death is not the death of the dead but of the living. "A Wounded Deer—leaps highest" in the "Extasy of *death*"; yet the next metaphors, the "*Smitten* Rock" and the "*trampled* Steel" are not death but, by anthropomorphic transfer, versions of that present anguish of which mirth is the cautious "Mail."

"It can't be 'Dying'! It's too Rouge—/The Dead shall go in White" is a poem ostensibly about a sunset, a traditional symbol for death; but, by the familiar figure of suggesting by denying, she has occasion to speak of a kind of death. The reference to white suggests Emily's own habitual garb from this time on. In the Orient, as she may have known, white is the color of lovers who have come through great tribulation and washed their robes (cf. no. 325 and Rev. 7:14). It is the color of her "blameless mystery"—perhaps in contrast to the blame-suspect black veil of Hawthorne's clergymen. White is the color for her kind of death-in-life; and the poem seems dynamized by it, with the sunset metaphor.

Suggestion by negation is most powerfully used in "It was not Death, for I stood up," a poem about death-in-life. This state deanimates the self.

> *The Figures I have seen*
> *Set orderly, for Burial,*
> *Reminded me, of mine—*
>
> *As if my life were shaven,*
> *And fitted to a frame,*
> *And could not breathe without a key. . . .*

It felt like the stopping of a clock, like frost-frozen ground (more deanimizing images); but most like chaos—chaos without "even a Report of Land—/To justify—Despair."

These poems about despair are probably the best poems Emily ever wrote; but they cannot be taken as her total "message to the world." Reading her work does not induce despair. For herself first, and then for her readers, the very articulation of despair is effectual movement toward its dispelling. And if anguish and fear paralyze, "self-reliance" has its resources unessayed without the felt need:

> *If your Nerve, deny you—*
> *Go above your Nerve—*
> *He can lean against the Grave,*
> *If he fear to swerve—*
>
> *'Tis so appalling—it exhilarates—*
> *So over Horror, it half Captivates—*
> *The Soul stares after it, secure—*
> *To know the worst, leaves no dread more—*

Then there are Emily's poems about immortality, which she both doubted and affirmed—affirmed not only on Bible testimony but from the argument that, as there are saints, there must be a Heaven—as there is grandeur, it cannot finally perish. These poems are variously mythic: there is no Biblical warrant for "fleshless lovers" meeting in Heaven. Whatever Emily's personal belief (centrally, a belief in belief), her after-death poems are readily translatable into other terms. As God is the resource, within or without, which transcends the resources we thought to be our limits, so eternity is a name for ultimate definitions—

> *When Sense from Spirit—files away—*
> *And Subterfuge—is done—*

The final sense of Emily's achievement is the power of poetry to register and master experience.

1957

The Marvels of M. R. James, Antiquary

I

Montague Rhodes James (1862–1938), successively provost of King's College, Cambridge, and provost of Eton, was that kind of English scholar who seems most alienly British to an American and whose happy immunities an American envies, seeing how much the fruition of his talents was possible only upon the allowance of his immunities.

It is difficult for an American to conceive of James as being offered—or even, if offered, as accepting and occupying —such honored posts. And indeed, his friend A. C. Benson already thinks the climate of the English university to be changing from its more indulgent and generous days. In his *Pater* (1906), he writes: "The praise of academical circles is reserved at the present time for people of brisk bursarial and business qualifications, of high technical accomplishment, for exact researchers, for effective teachers of prescribed subjects, for men of acute and practical minds, rather than for men of imaginative qualities."

James had, over Benson, the advantages of being an exact scholar and researcher; for the rest, however, he seems to have been allowed to follow his own line. He never married in order to provide King's with a hostess, nor in any other observable way deviated from his own natural path and tastes. No prudential calculations mar the integrity of the man and his career.

His father was rector of Livermere, a Suffolk village, only five miles from Bury St. Edmunds; and the boy had an early affection for the Abbey and the monks who read and wrote there. He was a bookish boy, drawn to the past of England and of Christendom in general. There is still extant his earliest work, a fourteen-page *Short Sketches of the Principal Northern Saints*, written in a severely historical style.

When he was sent to Eton, he was already interested in what became his scholarly work for life—Old, and especially New, Testament Apocryphal books. As a child he had a dream of opening a folio Bible and finding in it a book about the length of Obadiah, occupying a single page. "It was called," James writes in his memoirs, "the Book of Maher-Chalalhashbaz." While still at Eton, he spent his pocket money for a 'half' in buying four volumes of John Albert Fabricius' collections of the Old and New Testament Apocryphal Books. And when he came to consider what he should choose for a dissertation leading to a fellowship at King's, the obvious subject was something among the Apocryphal writings. "I had cherished for years, I still cherish, a quite peculiar interest in any document that has claimed to be a Book of the Bible, and is not." The reason given for this interest may seem somewhat odd, but James felt under no compulsion to explain.

After the Apocrypha, came another life-long interest—that in patristic and medieval manuscripts; and that taste, or pretaste, went even back of his Eton days to the library of his first school, Temple Grove, which contained Curzon's *Visits to the Monasteries of the Levant* (1849), with its account of monastic libraries.

Too myopic to engage in sports, and of esoteric interests, James was conscious of not being like the other boys. Yet he was well liked. As he himself wrote of Etonians, "they will not interfere with those who choose to walk in *byways*, so long as they are not asked to say that the eccentric is the only right-minded person . . . ; and so long as they are sure that singularity is not assumed in the hope of attracting attention."

In 1887 James was elected a fellow of King's and assistant

director of the Fitzwilliam Museum; in 1893, he became director of the Museum and dean of the College; he reduced sitting on committees to a minimum. He liked his work; and,
with his vast memory and extraordinary powers of concentrat-
ing, he could be at once leisurely and vastly 'productive.'

James had an early and lifelong gift of mimicry; and it
was in their boyhood at Livermere, their father's Suffolk parish, that he and his brother Herbert first devised the fictitious
characters of their impromptu dialogues. Herbert was Johnson,
a butcher, and Monty was a grocer called Barker, two rival
tradesmen given to mutual insinuations. "Barker would suggest
to Johnson that he tampered with his weights, to be accused in
turn of putting sand in his sugar." James could imitate all his
favorite Eton and King's friends, from his tutor and life-long
friend Luxmoore on.

Even in mature years, and in dignity of office, he indulged
his gift. Eton and King's were both founded by the fifteenth-
century King Henry VI—pious, a patron of learning, mur-
dered, regarded by many as a martyr. It was James who, centuries after, found in the Royal Chapel at Windsor the missing
bones of the martyr; who reverently wrapped them in silk and
reburied them. Yet when, as provost of Eton, he saw a small
group of visitors looking at a statue of Perseus in a college garden, and when, mistaken for a guide, he was asked whether this
was not a statue of the Founder, he replied, "Yes, this is a
statue of our Blessed Founder King Henry the Eighth; he is
'olding the 'ead of one of his wives. We don't know which it is,
but we think it must be Anne Boleyn."

He had a lifelong taste for Handel, for Anglican chants,
and English Church music, from Byrd to Boyce. As for literature, he knew the Psalms *in toto* and *verbatim*—presumably
both in the Prayer Book version (which is that of Coverdale)
and in the Vulgate; he was erudite in Dickens; and he was
more or less exhaustively read in nineteenth-century novels
and tales of the supernatural, notably those of Sheridan Le
Fanu, a collection of whose short stories he published in 1923.

In his Eton holidays, his tutor Luxmoore introduced him

to France. He traveled subsequently in Italy, Bavaria, Austria, Denmark; but France was his love, and from 1895 he made annual bicycling tours there, generally in April. He professed to have explored every *département* but one, and to have visited a hundred and forty-one cathedrals or remains of cathedrals.

I I

A ninety-six page book, *The Wanderings and Homes of Manuscripts*, which James published in 1919, is a little masterpiece of learning and of compression. Much of it modestly recounts the author's own discoveries; and all of it, however derived, is reviewed by a scholar entitled to an independent judgment. But it is not merely erudite and economical. The personality of the author, never obtrusive, is never absent. A sentence from the next to last paragraph is both fact and comment, the comment ultimately autobiographical.

"So it was," he writes, "that in reading Lambecius's eighteenth century catalogue of the Greek Mss. at Vienna I noted down an entry that seemed unusual; and some years after, when I had the opportunity of getting a friend in Vienna to look at the tract in question, it was found to be the unique copy of the most heretical (and therefore interesting) episode of the apocryphal Acts of St. John, written in the second century and copied, to our lasting astonishment and perplexity, by some honest orthodox cleric in the fourteenth." The "most heretical (and therefore interesting)" is a charming comment for an English scholar of the twentieth century to make in a scholarly book. James does not feel it necessary—here or elsewhere—to develop his statement.

The King James Bible (as well as the Vulgate and the Douai) includes a so-called Apocrypha, accepted as canonical by the Roman Church, half-accepted by the Anglican Church, rejected by Protestants: in this appendix to the Old Testament are some highly edifying books, *The Wisdom of Solomon* and *Ecclesiasticus*, also attributed to Solomon. But there are books considered canonical by no Church and included in no Bible: apocryphal works once attached to hallowed names—Enoch,

89

Abraham, Moses, the Apostles. And though James did not neglect the 'genuine' Apocrypha what really interested him was
that ultimate, the apocryphal apocrypha.

There is another genre dear to James, the apocalyptic—
works which uncover the covered, prophetic revelations of
Last Things. There is but one canonical Apocalypse, the book
called in the King James Bible the Revelation of St. John the
Divine; but considerable in number are the apocryphal apocalypses—obviously doubly interesting, for they claim to reveal
the unrevealed and yet are uncanonical; some of them are Jewish and some are heretically Christian—and some are mixtures
of the Jewish and the Christian, and some are Gnostic.

There are apocalypses attached to the names of Ezra, Ba-
ruch, and Abraham, prerabbinic Palestinian-Jewish; in his *Lost
Apocrypha of the Old Testament*, James collects up fragments
of Apocalypses attributed to Adam, Moses, Elijah, and Zeph-
aniah which have survived in the writings of the Christian
Fathers, notably the Alexandrians, Clement and Origen.

Why should one be so interested in these writings which,
after critical examination and sifting, have been discarded?
James, it is to be conjectured, shared the "generous belief" of
Pico della Mirandola (and of Walter Pater, writing of Pico),
that "nothing which had ever interested the human mind could
wholly lose its vitality"—even though, to quote Pater again, it
should seem "a curiosity of the human mind, a 'madhouse-cell,'
if you will." James, too, I conjecture, felt sympathy for those
anonymous seers who, sheltering themselves under the sanction
of some hallowed name, aspired to add some words of prophetic insight, to expound some doctrine to them so urgent as
to seem revealed. Like William James, Montague James doubtless thought truth revealed not only to communally authorized
exponents—Doctors of the Synagogue and the Church, professors of theology and philosophy, but—in gleams and glimpses
at least—to fanatics and cranks.

On a humbler level, restitution of things lost is a form of
detective work, possessing all the interest which attaches to
detection; and yet it has the status of 'scholarship.' The merit

of research lies in its difficulty; its fun in solving a puzzle—
finding a solution after the application of assorted strategies.
'Research' is viewed in the academic world as something meri-
torious to whatever it is applied: it is designated "a contribution to learning." Work it certainly is, even though it would
often seem, and always when mechanically pursued, 'busy-
work' for grown-up children, paper industry.

No one appears to have questioned James about the reasons for his fascination with the apocryphal and heretical and
apocalyptic—any more than about his expert fondness for cata-
loguing pre-Reformation manuscripts in the college libraries of
Oxford and Cambridge; and there remains no indication that
James ever questioned his own subterranean motives.

Sir Thomas Browne confesses to have held in his green
youth to some two or three heresies, "not begotten in the latter centuries but old and obsolete,—such as could never have
been revived but by such extravagant and irregular heads as
mine." Had Dr. M. R. James held any heresies, surely they, too,
would have been old and obsolete ones. He happened to live in
latitudinarian days in which the Anglican Church was tolerant
of deviations from orthodoxy. But James passed certainly for
an orthodox enough gentleman and scholar, neither High nor
Low nor Modernist, but, as the British phrase has it, a 'central
Churchman.' He preached sermons in the chapels of King's
College and Eton. He was constantly the host, or the guest, of
bishops and deans. He was fond of churches; a scholar in the
history of organs and organ cases, pre-Reformation stained
glass, and frescoes and statues; fond and knowing of the Bible
and the Prayer Book.

Yet he was not, clearly, a ritualist in the pejorative sense of
the word. His interest was in the 'old things,' in the continui-
ties of civilization—European, and especially English. In the
title of his first volume of short stories he calls himself an 'antiquary'—putting himself into a long line of Britons—Camden,
Dugdale, Cotton, Ritson, Sir Walter Scott. Lovers of 'old
things' are sad at the way Progress demolishes all the monuments—and the miniatures, too—which call the past, and conti-

nuity, to our remembrance. For mankind ignorant of its past is like a man without memory, condemned to live in the flux of Now. "Remove not the ancient landmarks" (Prov. 22:28).

III

James was a scholar, not a philosopher, theorist, or even concerned justifier and rationalizer of his own professional work. A friend tells a characteristic anecdote: once asked why he was interested in some particular piece of research, his spontaneous answer was, "Why is any one interested in anything?" The implication is that no interest can be very deeply rationalized; that interests are their own justification to the interested —a view inimical to any attempt at constructing a hierarchy of values among intellectual activities. His was the view of the specialist, who makes no effort to see his work in relation to that of others; who says, "I work at what fascinates me; let others do the same."

When he was not doing 'research,' James read novels, the latest, or old favorites like those of Dickens and Le Fanu. And, during the years when he was dean and later provost of King's and at the height of his activities as Apocryphal scholar and cataloguer of manuscripts in college and cathedral libraries, he was writing stories, scholarly and horrific stories, of the occult, the first volume of which, *Ghost Stories of an Antiquary*, appeared in 1904. The two-fold nature of his publications was wittily recognized by the Public Orator of Oxford. Presenting James for an honorary doctorate in 1927, he characterized the honored as a scholar who, "ex omni scrinio, armaria, fenestra, pariete, cryptoporticu litterarum atque artium miracula, ne dicam lamiarum monstra et terricula in lucem protulit."

The two activities were ostensibly, and something more than ostensibly, linked together by the fact that the tales were such as an antiquary might tell. Not that they are literally by-products of his scholarly researches—as Andrew Lang's Blue and Red Fairy Tale books might be said of Lang's, or the Grimm brothers' *Märchen* of theirs: James makes it clear that almost all of the "ostensible erudition" in his tales is "pure invention." But it takes a scholar to invent such plausibly ostensible erudition as James's.

The question with what relative seriousness James took his modes of utterance is engaging to a critic, but of no concern to James. He was shy and taciturn when it came to speaking in his own person; was voluble and eloquent, his friends say, only when he was impersonating someone else, when he was speaking through a mask. Thus, his one really disappointing performance is *Eton and Kings*, a sizable book written at a publisher's request; for despite a few factual statements about his own activities the book is less autobiography than a collection of reminiscences of tutors and classmates, school and college jokes, anecdotes reduced to allusion, flat and pointless to any outside the family circle and when deprived of the impersonating voice. The scholar in him is bound to a kind of literal accuracy. He is not, as he would be in a fiction, free to indulge in plausibilities and imagined possibilities. What he thought of narrative fiction, the art of plausible invention, can only be conjectured. Did he think of it as mere entertainment, diversion from research, or as having some form of truth and seriousness peculiar to itself? Or (*dulce et utile*) as combining both, in a mode not, by a gentleman, to be pressed for definition? Presumably this last.

Just how James came to be a writer of tales is unclear, except that it began with oral storytelling. He told stories to the choirboys of King's College on Christmas eve, as later he read many of his tales, often completed just in time, to his friends, also on Christmas eve.

The Christmas season was, in England, the appropriate time for ghost stories. One thinks of Dickens' annual Christmas books. And Henry James's "Turn of the Screw" was supplied for similar use: when, he writes in a preface, "I was asked for something seasonable by the promoters of a periodical dealing with the time-honored Christmas-tide toy, I bethought myself at once of the vividest little note for sinister romance that I had ever jotted down." Curious that Christmas eve should be the occasion for tellers of ghost stories; but we read in *Hamlet*

93

that, "some say," at the hallowed season the cock sings all
night.

> *And then, they say, no spirit dare stir abroad . . .*
> *No fairy takes, nor witch hath power to charm . . .*

Perhaps, by forgotten tradition, the telling of ghost stories
is then not only safe but even a form both of defiance and
thanksgiving.

James's ghost stories were written between 1894 and 1927;
were published in four volumes, beginning with *Ghost Stories
of an Antiquary* (1904); and the four volumes were assembled
in 1931 as *Collected Ghost Stories*. In his chary Preface, their
author refused to explain "how I came to write them," avowing
that, as they were said to have "given pleasure of a certain
sort" to readers, he had attained his "whole object in writing
them"—a statement unlikely to be the whole truth about any
author. There are other motives for writing than doing so for
money (according to Dr. Johnson, the only reason why a sensible man would thus exert himself), or for fame, or to entertain readers; and James presumably derived a certain sort of
pleasure from writing his tales, and expressing an otherwise
unexpressible part of himself.

He did write an Introduction to *Ghosts and Marvels*
(1924), a collection of 'uncanny' tales issued by the Oxford
Press in its 'World's Classics' series. The choice of writers and
tales, which ranges from Defoe through George Eliot to Algernon Blackwood, and includes his own "Casting of the Runes,"
was, for some reason, not left to James, who felt therefore the
more free to comment. "Schalken the Painter" is singled out
both as "one of the best of Le Fanu's good things" and as con-
forming to James's "own ideals" for the ghost story better
than some of the others.

And Sheridan Le Fanu was, indeed, James's especial favorite among his predecessors. He spent considerable time tracking down the writings of Le Fanu in the periodicals—usually the
Dublin University Magazine, in which most of them, many of
them anonymously, appeared. In 1923 he published a selection

from them, *Madam Crowl's Ghost and Other Tales of Mystery*, writing in his Preface: Le Fanu "stands absolutely in the first rank as a writer of ghost stories. That is my deliberate verdict, after reading all the supernatural tales I have been able to get hold of. Nobody sets the scene better than he, nobody touches in the effective detail more deftly."

It is customary to describe Dr. James's tales as in the tradition of Le Fanu, the founder of the British succession, as Poe is of the American; the resemblance is not, however, close. Le Fanu had a wider range of themes and styles; and he wrote a few really powerful pieces—notably "Carmilla," his vampire story, and "Schalken" for another, probably "Mr. Justice Harbottle," and possibly "Green Tea." He was an educated gentleman with a sense of history; but, by comparison with James, he lacks method (possibly the reason why he is less readily appreciable by an American reader). He lacked James's sense of humor, his gift at vernacular dialogue, and his distinction of narrative style. But, as any anthology will show, there is scarcely a British author who has not at some time or other written a story of the occult; and to read through the collection, *Ghosts and Marvels*, or Summers' *A Supernatural Omnibus*, is to see how Le Fanu emerges as the first specialist or professional. Certain it is that James's admiration for him has been shared by other subsequent British specialists like Summers and Dorothy Sayers, who undertook a biography of Le Fanu, left unfinished.

The only two Americans in the collection are Poe and Hawthorne. James makes it clear that "Ligeia," "which in many people's judgment . . . ranks as a classic," does not in his; and "Young Goodman Brown," assuredly a masterpiece, he passes by without comment. The American tradition of the supernatural, the American Gothic, lies outside of his sympathy, almost certainly as too 'psychological'—as placing the emphasis not upon intruding, objectively existing spirits, but upon the ghost-seers, the hauntable, upon those who see their shadows, their repressed or otherwise other selves, who project their guilt and their terror.

It is the distinction of "The House of Usher," among Poe's tales, that in it the narrator, with whom normal readers may relatively identify, enters the doomed house from without, and, at its end, gets back over the drawbridge into a mundane reality, the reader escaping with him. But in Poe's tales generally, whether told in the first person ("Men call me mad," says Aegeus) or in the third, the chief person is highly neurotic if not completely mad; and the incestuous stories involve twin *personae*—the mad Ligeia is seen by the mad narrator. Others (like "The Black Cat") are told by the hallucinatorily persecuted. And Hawthorne's "Young Goodman Brown" more than admits it must be said, of a purely psychological interpretation.

The 'ghostly stories,' as Edel calls them, of Henry James (an author not included in *Ghosts and Marvels*, and never mentioned by the other James) have as their chief character—even if we chose to reject the widely current interpretation of "The Turn of the Screw"—someone hauntable. The horror, real and powerful as it is in "The Jolly Corner," is subjectively horrible; only the particular person who returns to his old home can see the maimed, aggressive self he sees. And consider "The Friend of the Friends" and "Maud-Evelyn."

Montague James's ghosts are those of people who in their lives were set apart—witches, wizards, unjust judges, specialists, and traffickers in the occult. But those to whom they, or their effects, appear are themselves ordinary sensible people—"patients," to use his own word—with whom the reader can identify: indeed, only for a here and now normal reader can there be a real supernatural.

This is James's special note and method; and, in a few paragraphs of his introduction to *Ghosts and Marvels*, he is uncommonly and delightfully explicit about how properly to handle the "small and special" *genre*. As for time, he writes: "The detective story cannot be too much up-to-date: the motor, the telephone, the aeroplane, the newest slang, are all in place there. For the ghost story, a slight haze of distance is desirable. 'Thirty years ago,' 'Not long before the war,' are very proper openings. . . . On the whole, I think that a setting so modern that the ordinary reader can judge of its naturalness for himself is preferable to anything antique. For some degree of actuality is the charm of the best ghost stories; not a very insistent actuality but one strong enough to allow the reader to identify himself with the patient. . . ."

As for the "atmosphere," he remarks, "Let us, then, be introduced to the actors in a placid way; let us see them going about their ordinary business undisturbed by forebodings, pleased with their surroundings; and into this calm environment let the ominous thing put out its head, unobtrusively at first, and then more insistently, until it holds the stage"—an admirable account of his own method. He adds that sometimes a loophole may be left for a natural explanation of the horrendous, "but, I would say, let the loophole be so narrow as not to be quite practicable." Here, however, he is being reluctantly permissive of the practice of others; for it is impossible to think of any James story in which finally, and after preliminary possible ambiguities, there is any naturalistic interpretation, including the psychological, which is left available.

How far the Antiquary himself believed in ghosts is a matter of conjecture. Asked the question, he replied, "I am prepared to consider evidence and accept it if it satisfies me." It may be surmised that he was neither a dogmatic believer like the Reverend Montague Summers, that prolific and credulous author of books on all manner of uncanny things, witches, werewolves and vampires, nor yet a "Sadducee," a dogmatic disbeliever, like the positivist Professor of Ontography in "Whistle and I'll Come to You My Lad."

In his intermediate position, involving at least the temporary suspension of disbelief, he found, as a narrativist, help by invoking 'tradition,' that hallowed intermediary between fact and fiction, or history and theology. He had tried, he half-jocosely observes, to make his ghosts act in "ways not inconsistent with the rules of folklore." What are these alleged rules? Let us construct some out of memory. There are no happy *revenants*. Ghosts are unquiet spirits, keeping their fantasmic life

because they have either suffered some evil which must be re-
venged or perpetrated some evil for which they must suffer, or
because they are earthbound by obsessive concern with their
earthly interest—classically (as in the "Abbot Thomas" story)
their buried treasure. They haunt the place where once they
lived (a limitation James sometimes violates); they appear between midnight and cockcrow, either in the white of the burial shroud or in the garb habitually worn in the flesh. How are
they to be dispelled? Sometimes, having had their revenge,
they are satiated. Sometimes they tire of their watch; appear
less and less frequently, till they fade away. Sometimes they
can be confined, driven into a cupboard, a barrel, or a bottle—a
procedure to be undertaken by the clergy, with their books of
Latin and their exorcisms—though of course the clergy, if
scholars, are also peculiarly liable to *libido sciendi* and the use
of magic. Ghosts can sometimes be kept from wandering by
driving a stake through their bodies, a precaution taken with
the bodies of suicides, or by burning the body.

Local legends of supernatural happenings James does not
use; but the sense of locality is highly significant in his stories.
The British annexation of India made accessible to English authors the possibility of introducing the occult as at a plausible
distance; but James's tales (unless laid, as a few are, in nearby
France, Sweden, or Denmark) are English in setting.

It is places, not persons, which are hauntable; and rather
the country than the city. Places are haunted by their own
past, their own history. Britain is haunted by its successive invasions, successive stratifications of cultures: the Celts, the An-
glo-Saxons, the Romans, the Normans; by its successive religions—Druidic, Celtic Christian, Roman Christian, and, in
alternations, Catholic, Anglican, Puritan, Catholic, Anglican.
The vanquished peoples and religions are never completely ex-
tirpated. The overturned and overthrown and outmoded lie
beneath the surface or at the periphery, waiting. The latest
culture temporarily tops its predecessors, as excavation—literal
or imaginative, historical or psychological—unearths layer after
layer. Fragments of past grandeur, Druidic circles and Roman

baths and temples survive to mock modern hopes of being the last as well as the latest.

Such a strain dimly echoes Browne's *Urn Burial,* doubtless the greatest poem an antiquary ever wrote—at least an English antiquary. But the sense of the past is, with every antiquary, bound up with things, places, local attachments.

IV

The stories are all meticulously and lovingly framed in time as well as localized in setting. For time in his tales, James has at sensitive command the centuries from the Middle Ages (and their medieval Latin) on; he empathizes their concerns, their view of the world. Our antiquary can veraciously imitate their literary styles, whether of letter writing or journals, or, in more and dignified urbanity, of sermons and contributions to the *Gentleman's Magazine.*

The antiquary and the mimic combine in the delight, and the skill, with which James varies the time of his stories. The time is often double: the traditional device of the discovery and reading *now* of some document written in the remote or more recent past.

Thus "The Stalls of Barchester Cathedral" opens with an obituary notice which a recent cataloguer of manuscripts for a college library reads in the obituary section of the *Gentleman's Magazine* for 1818, in which Archdeacon Haynes is elegantly characterized: "His sermons, ever conformable to the principles of the religion and Church which he adorned, displayed in no ordinary degree, without the least trace of enthusiasm, the refinement of the scholar united with the graces of the Christian." The antiquary then discovers in the library of the college to which Haynes belonged a tin box of the Haynes papers, bequeathed by his sister; and from the mysteriously deceased archdeacon's letters and diary extracts are quoted. The explanation of the strange death belongs to the narrating antiquary.

"Count Magnus" purports to be written on the basis of papers which came into the narrator's hands, he will not tell how—papers collected for the composition of a travel book, "such a volume as was a common product of the [eighteen] forties and fifties. Horace Marryat's *Journal of a Resident in Jutland and the Danish Isles* [a fictitious book by a fictitious author] is a fair specimen of the class to which I allude." "The Treasure of the Abbot Thomas" concerns an antiquary of the mid-nineteenth century who is started on his quest by reading, in an eighteenth-century Latin history of a German abbey dissolved after the French Revolution, the life of an abbot who dies early in the sixteenth century. "The Diary of Mr. Poynter" recounts the twentieth-century discovery at a London book auction of a 1710 diary, the author a fictive member of the circle of Oxford antiquaries centered on Thomas Hearne; and in the diary, under the date of 1707, Poynter has written:

"Old Mr. Casbury, of Acrington, told me this day much of young Sir Everard Charlett. . . . This Charlett was a personable young gent., but a loose atheistical companion, and a great Lifter, as they then call'd the hard drinkers. . . . He was a very beautiful person, and constantly wore his own Hair, which was very abundant, from which, and his loose way of living, the cant name for him was Absalom, and he was accustom'd to say that indeed he believ'd he had shortened old David's days, meaning his father, Sir Job Charlett, an old worthy cavalier."

James has confessed that some of his stories were suggested by specific places, in France, Denmark, and England. In pre-Reformation stained glass, wall-painting, sculpture, organs and organ cases, and choir screens, he had especial expertness; like his friend A. C. Benson, he had a fondness for Jacobean and Restoration fittings as well as for medieval. In "The Stalls of Barchester Cathedral" and again in "An Episode of Cathedral History," he expresses, once in his own person, his distaste for the work of the Gothic Revival. "When you enter the choir of Barchester Cathedral now, you pass through a screen of metal and colored marbles, designed by Sir Gilbert Scott, and find yourself in what I must call a very bare and odiously furnished place." "There was a lot of lovely stuff went then, sir," says the verger of the destruction and purification which preceded the choir's restoration to its former hypothetical state. "Crool it was . . . all that beautiful wainscot oak, as good as the day it was put up, and garlands-like of foliage and fruit, and lovely old gilding work on the coats of arms and the organ pipes." Then there are the elaborate descriptions, in "Count Magnus," of the seventeenth-century Swedish church with adjoining mausoleum and in "An Uncommon Prayer-Book," the seventeenth-century private Royalist chapel.

For his domestic architecture, there may be cited the opening of "The Ash Tree":

"Everyone who has travelled over Eastern England knows the smaller country-houses with which it is studded—the rather dank little buildings, usually in the Italian style, surrounded with parks of some eighty to a hundred acres. For me they have always had a very strong attraction: with the grey paling of split oak, the noble trees, the meres with their reed-beds, and the line of distant woods. Then I like the pillared portico —perhaps stuck on to a red-brick Queen Anne house which has been faced with stucco to bring it into line with the 'Grecian' taste of the end of the eighteenth century. . . ."

There is another and differently constituted framing of the *Ghost Stories*, one which no single story completely exemplifies but which is the pervasive pattern. This framing is partly a matter of social classes. The outermost framework is that of the educated and socially well-placed—which is either the world in which James lived, the world of scholars, of professors and fellows and the cathedral clergy, or the world he well knew—that of the landed gentry—good, cultivated, sensible gentlefolk. These, persons not easily hauntable, are the "patients" of his tales. They are such persons as Dr. and Mrs. Ashton of Whitminster or the Anstruthers of Westfield Hall, Essex, in "The Rose Garden," with their golf, their gardenings, and their sketching, or antiquarians like Dennistoun of Cambridge.

Then there is the world of the various lower classes, carefully distinguished: butlers and managers of estates, housekeepers, innkeepers, clerks, vergers, and other guides, peasants. The characters in this repertory are all, one may suppose, variants of Johnson and Barker, the butcher and the grocer of 'Monty's' boyhood and boyish dialogue with his brother; but, with his masterly mimicry, James discriminates many characteristic kinds of speech. He took most pleasure, it would seem, in that of the half-educated—those who, by their habitual association as aids to scholars and gentlefolk, collect scraps of Latin and polysyllabic words and other misplaced adornments. These delightful people, though (like Miss Bates, in *Emma*, whom James mentions) they are copious of utterance, are hard to extricate from the stories in which they flourish; but one of the choicest, certainly, is Mr. Cooper, the bailiff of "Mr. Humphreys and His Inheritance"—Mr. Cooper, who describes the heir's uncle as "a complete, thorough valentudinarian" and describes himself as of a summer sleeping *"in status quo."*

Lower down, and farther away, and rather indicated than directly presented are 'peasants,' rustics, country folk. They constitute a kind of chorus; and their function is to keep alive the traditions of supernatural visitations which, remembered by at least the oldest inhabitant of a village, they are reluctant to confess, lest they be laughed at by the city modernists. 'Yet there is always,' it is a kind of motto for the *Ghost Stories*, 'something in what country people say'—something at peril disregarded.

Thus, gradually, by the pleasurably winding road which leads into the stories—the time, the place, the normal and living, we reach their eruptive center—the horror, about the nature of which something explicit must be said.

There are verses in the thirty-fourth chapter of Isaiah (one of them James cites in a tale) which picture the horror of desolation—the wasted land inhabited by cormorants and bitterns and owls and dragons. "The wild beasts of the desert shall also meet with the wild beasts of the field, and the satyr shall cry to his fellow: the screech owl also shall rest there . . .' then shall the vultures also be gathered, every one with her mate."

Except for the *satyr*, a mysterious word which means either a compound of man and ape, or the *lamia*, that famous monster in half human shape which sucks the blood of children, these are all traditional *natural* objects of human aversion, beasts and birds of ill omen associated with death and the devouring of dead bodies. In James's stories, owls, bats, and rats and spiders, the traditionally ominous creatures of the night are frequent. But more terrifying than the literal creatures are their properties, operating of themselves: multiple tentacles, for example, which reach out and entwine themselves stranglingly about the human intruder.

Hair is invoked in double signification: often the creatures are described as having their arms or what pass for their bodies covered with gray or grisly hair; a hairy man is a primitive like the Ainus of Japan; he recalls our anthropoid ancestry. But then there is another, opposite but equally repellent, signification of hair: the effeminate long hair of Sir Everard Charlett, the long hair of Absalom, the King's son, who was caught by his hair as he rode horseback through the forest, who was hanged by his own hair. The wallpaper made from a stuff pattern of Sir Everard's hair, the rippling lines, the almost curling waves of tresses, have their serpentine terror, their menace of entanglement. These are the rival fears of the primitive and the decadent.

More characteristic of James's terrors is the terror of the amorphous. In "Whistle and I'll Come to You, My Lad," the only tale which incorporates one of James's own dreams, the presumed figure of a Knight Templar, perhaps of the fourteenth century, materializes itself out of "the bed-clothes of which it had made itself a body": the living spectator's face; and, as he looks, he sees the face of the other, "an intensely horrible face of *crumpled linen*." So, analogously, comes, at the end of "The Uncommon Prayer-Book," a roll of white flannel, four or five feet high, with a kind of face in the upper end of it, the face earth-covered, the eyes, "much as if there were two big spiders' bodies in the holes." It falls from a safe where the venomous prayer book has been stored; and, falling, it inflicts a serpent-like bite which kills the dealer who had stolen it from a seventeenth-century chapel dedicated to a Royalist's sole object of passion—the hatred of Oliver Cromwell.

Ghosts, as commonly conceived of—white, visual images —rarely appear, and then at some distance. More frequently they are heard in cries, moans, or (more disturbing yet) whispers and murmurs; or their presence in a room, or a landscape, is felt. When, however, the evil dead are menaced, they come close and grow heavy. James rarely uses the word 'nightmare,' and then not with technical accuracy, yet his chiefest horror is some version of the incubus—something partly human, partly animal, partly *thing* which presses down, grasps and grips, threatens to strangle or suffocate, a heavy weight of palpable materiality—not 'psychic' but sensually gross—a recall not of shroud but of corpse, of a living dead or death.

Thus, the Abbot Thomas, at the bottom of the well, guarding his treasure bags, is an *it* as well as a *he*. "It hung for an instant on the edge of the hole, then slipped forward on to my chest, and *put its arms around my neck.* . . . I was conscious of a most horrible smell of mold, and of a cold kind of face pressed against my own, and moving slowly over it, and of several—I don't know how many—legs or arms or tentacles or something clinging to my body." That night, the creature of darkness—its sounds and its odor—pervaded the narrator's hotel; and it was relief indeed when daybreak came and he and his servant were able to put the slab of stone back over the well and what inhabited it.

v

The tales of Dr. James are a continuing delight. Indeed, they are so rich in detail, and told with such seemingly artless art, that it is only upon repeated readings that they are properly cherished—so far are they from being mere shockers the pleasure of which is exhausted after the first blunt impact is spent. They have, indeed, to be read closely, for they are to be read for their surface as well as their structure—so far as these two can be disengaged.

James is the author of much more than a few anthology

pieces. The two commonly included, "Casting the Runes" and "Whistle and I'll Come to You, My Lad," are both excellent stories and excellent James stories; but the level is extraordinarily high. Of the thirty included in *Collected Ghost Stories*, there are, say, eighteen others as good, some of them better. A list of the best should include "Lost Hearts," "The Ash Tree," "No. 13," "Count Magnus," "The Rose Garden," "The Stalls of Barchester Cathedral," "Mr. Humphreys and His Inheritance," "The Residence at Whitminster," "The Diary of Mr. Poynter," "An Episode of Cathedral History," "A Disappearance and an Appearance," "The Haunted Dolls' House," "The Uncommon Prayer-Book," "A View from a Hill," and "An Evening's Entertainment." Even this narrowing down has required sacrifices; for it must be said that in every story of James there are touches, 'passage-work,' phrasings not to be missed. And, for his reader who has the tastes of a scholar, there is the recreative research of tracking down his allusions, which, according to his scholarly fancy, are sometimes genuine and sometimes feigned—to discover whether there was a minor Greek author called Polyaenus or a seventeenth-century English organ builder named Dallas, or even to learn what Dr. Blimber really said in Chapter XII of *Dombey and Son*.

This last item (*Collected Stories*, 124 and note) is one of Dr. James's own extranarratorial touches, discoverable upon close examination of the stories. He does not hesitate to appear in his own person, either in stories told in the third person or by a feigned narrator. Strictness of 'point of view' is no fetish of his. Yet such are his lowness of pitch and ease of manner (both despite the *horrendum* which awaits us) that no desirable illusion is shattered. He is a born storyteller with no sense of shame at being one—no sense of 'stories' as undignified or even untrue because they are not 'history.' Born storytellers are oral storytellers, and the sound of the storyteller's voice as well as of the many mimicked voices is heard in all James's writing; it not only abounds in dialogue but is itself speech pleased with the resources of speech.

Within the limits of their genre, James's stories have very

considerable range and variety, both of theme and treatment, scarcely to be conveyed by defining in a phrase given to each what they are 'about.' There are several stories about the wicked Judge Jeffreys, the 'hanging judge' who was lord chancellor under James II and died in the Tower of London, with phrases and images drawn from the State Trials, which were of Hawthorne's reading as well as James's: at the end of one, the parsons of the neighborhood are summoned to drive a stake to imprison the wandering guilty spirit of the judge. There is a story of a hung witch, whose vengeance follows her judge and his heirs till the ash tree in which she lived as a spider is burned down; and one about a *lamia* which escapes from its tomb in a cathedral, and another about a cathedral prebendary and archdeacon who contrived the death of his predecessor and who was in turn killed by the ghosts of the predecessor, aided by a tomcat, one of the grotesque sculptures on his cathedral stall which had been carved of wood from the Hanging Oak and come to life. One is about a Royalist lady who had issued an illicit Prayer Book with provision for celebrating Cromwell's birthday by prayer for his death, and another about a grasping lady landowner who removes the ancient landmark in order to extend her own estate. There is a story ("A View from a Hill") about a pair of field glasses "filled and sealed" with a distillation of dead men's bones through which one can see a Priory town and a gallows which existed only in the past. There is in the story about Count Magnus, a vampire Swedish nobleman who made the black Pilgrimage and who, escaping from his tomb, pursues to England and kills the traveler who let his spirit loose; and there is another story about a Danish hotel room 13, which vanishes except by night, when it is then haunted by a magician who has sold his soul to Satan. And, finally, there are tales concerning pre-Christian and pagan mysteries—Mithraism and the Druids—and the Templars, and the Italianate Englishman, who, with the aid of an Italian, builds the maze and Satanic sundial which are Mr. Humphreys' "Inheritance."

Such an enumeration not only inadequately conveys what

the stories are about; it also gives a misleading impression of the *Ghost Stories* as a museum of "Gothic" horrors, which it is not. It does, however, properly demonstrate the use to Dr. James's subtle fictions of something crude and violent as their matrix. There must be some gross, refractory matter to withstand the counterforce of refinement, of carving and polishing.

The ghost stories of Montague James have their rightful place in the final chapter of recent books on the tradition of the Gothic Romance. Even such parts of its 'machinery' as the gloomy old press with its secrets, James can use, with the affectionate, half-parodic bow of an antiquarian. But he is the master of a new and probably inimitable mode in his special combination of erudition, dry, precise, rather donnish style, realistic dialogue, humor, and treatment of the supernatural—a supernatural never explained away but variously interpreted by characters dramatically differentiated. He has common sense, and uncommon, too.

[*1969*]

A. C. Benson and His Friends

In 1926, a year after the death of Arthur Christopher Benson,
there was published a memorial volume called *Benson as Seen
by Some Friends*. It might appear that there is little more to
say of Benson and his busy life after his friends have finished
with him: I say 'Friends' without ironic intent, for the British
can like, respect, even love their friends without feeling it necessary to suppress mention of their friends' difficulties, lacks,
eccentricities, lapses. And, as the lengthy obituaries in the London *Times* show, this candid portraiture is deemed appropriate
to the great as well as the picturesquely odd. Indeed, we are
intended to find greatness of some kind implied by the rigor of
the criticism.

Benson's friends, who are as outspoken as they mean to be
just, liked the man and his company, even loved him; but they
could not like the books by which he was most widely known
—books from which he had excluded (with imperfect awareness, it would appear) three-fourths of himself. He was fond
of writing; he wrote easily; he cared above all things to be a
writer: these things were for him enough. His friends saw his
writing as an indulgence, and thought he had mistaken his role
in life; and one or two of them clearly said so.

Arthur Benson came from one of those ecclesiastical, academic, and writing families which appear so characteristic of
England, at least until recently. He began life with distinct advantages, as the eldest surviving son of Edward White Benson,
successively headmaster of Wellington College (a 'public

school'), canon of Lincoln, first bishop of Truro, and arch-bishop of Canterbury. And he himself was educated at Eton and King's College, Cambridge; in 1885, he returned to Eton as a master, remaining there for nearly twenty years.

Windsor Castle is the close neighbor of Eton College: it is from the Castle Terrace that one has the best "prospect" of Eton. Through Dr. Davidson, dean of the Royal Chapel, who had married the daughter of Archbishop Tait and who had earlier been chaplain to Benson's father, the young master had access to the "Windsor circle." And, until the death of his father in 1896, he had also, as he says, opportunities of meeting "a good many of the leading personalities of the day". . . during "the tranquil and prosperous period covering the closing years of Queen Victoria's reign." It should be added that Benson's younger brothers were both writers well known in their time: Edward Frederick, novelist (author of *Dodo*) and co-pious memoirist, and Robert Hugh, Catholic monsignor and novelist: to popular writers about the Edwardian period, the Benson brothers appear as something of a team.

The most dramatic event in Arthur Benson's quiet life was his departure in 1905, from Eton, where he had been both pupil and master—a break which left him with such bitterness that he refused to return till shortly before his death. He had resigned his mastership in order to devote himself solely to writing, to literature; the bitterness was partly the conse-quence of his not having been offered the headmastership (which he both did and didn't want, but wanted offered—as subsequently he wanted positions of prestige and responsibility offered without being sure that he wanted to accept), but chiefly, it would seem, a resentment of the teacher's crowded and exacting schedule which had kept him—not from writing, but from writing as much as exemption would have allowed.

At forty, then, shaking off the dust of Eton, he betook himself to Cambridge, was soon offered an honorary fellow-ship at the smallest college, Magdalene (of which subsequently he became master), and gave himself over to literature. At Eton, he had, at the instigation of the Royal Family, begun the editing of Queen Victoria's Diary, but he had been, as a writer, chiefly the writer of thin, graceful, accomplished, end of the century verse. Now he began the prodigious output which he continued to the end of his life, writing far more than even a popular author could publish.

Partly, probably, in order to justify himself for his early retirement from teaching, Benson wrote down in his Journals for August 1905 a list of what he had produced since leaving Eton: "1. *Cambridge Revisited* (not published); 2. *FitzGerald* [English Men of Letters series], (62,200 words); 3. *Upton Letters* (80,000); 4. *College Window* (40,000); 5. *Pater* [*also* EML series], (60,000); 6. *Leonard* [published under the title *Beside Still Waters*], (60,000); 7. My poetry lectures—quite a book (50,000); 8. *The Thread of Gold* (80,000); 9. Enough essays and articles to form a small volume of themselves (40,000); 10. I have published a book of poems"—all this in addition to continued work at the Diary of the Queen.

In 1906 Benson published his most popular and famous book, *From a College Window*. It was composed of essays most of which had earlier appeared in the *Cornhill Magazine* —some sample topics are: "Books," "On Growing Older," "Conversation," "Beauty," "Education," "The Criticism of Others," "The Simple Life." A few of these are topics treated by Emerson; but the treatment could scarcely be more dissimilar. Unlike Emerson—and indeed unlike Charles Lamb on the same subject, Benson on books mentions no specific book by name: his concern is with the 'pleasure of reading' and the uplifting influence of this pleasure.

These are 'familiar' and 'personal essays'; indeed, the personal pronoun is ubiquitous; so, too, are all words antonymic to the abstract and the general and objective, to the dogmatic, assertive, or matter of fact. The sentences begin, "I think," "I feel," "I like to feel," "I have sometimes thought that"; they are parenthetically punctuated with such seemingly unassertive phrases. One essay opens with: "I cannot help wishing sometimes that English people had more theories about conversation. Really good talk is one of the greatest pleasures there is, and yet how rarely one comes across it." The essay on "Art," a discussion, naturally for Benson, of the artist, reminds the reader that "whether one be of the happy number or not who have the haunting instinct for some special form of expression, one may learn at all events to deal with life in an artistic spirit. I do not at all mean by that that one should learn to overvalue the artistic side of life, to hold personal emotion to be a finer thing than unselfish usefulness." And so on.

These essays vaguely recall the "Apology for Idlers" and other essays of Stevenson's. Their line goes back, indeed, to Hazlitt and Lamb, perhaps chiefly Lamb; but to invoke these old Romantic masters of the 'familiar essay,' so long out of style, is to contrast their firmness and delicacy with Benson's dilution and genteel vulgarization of this genre. The specifically Bensonian *persona* is the cultivated yet kindly and very human College Don; the Bensonian mixture adds to the confessional note the gentle gospel of ethical aestheticism; the tone is that of 'thoughtfulness' uninformed by intellection.

From a College Window did not meet with the approval of Benson's old Eton tutor, Luxmoore, whose epistolary comment runs: "Thin, very thin; pleasantly written . . . ; but I have read it only in scraps. A.C.B. has spoilt himself by rapid writing and thin thinking. . . . I hope he will stop writing for a long time and do a lot of energetic and unpleasant things to take his attention off of himself."

But the book had an immediate and long-continued success. It was important enough to be parodied by Max Beerbohm (*A Christmas Garland*) and by *Punch* ("I often think how much the postman does for us and how little we do for the postman"). And, in the course of time, summer tourists visited Magdalene requesting to be shown the very college window through which the Don looked out upon the world.

Such success would be difficult to resist. Moreover, Benson enjoyed writing these "thin, pleasant" meditations. Accordingly, the book criticized by his friends was followed by *Beside Still Waters, The Thread of God, The Altar Fire, The House of Quiet*, and many more. They went into large editions, were read all over the English-reading world: their tone, with its blend of the familiar essayist and the lay preacher, made his readers feel that a cultivated and sympathetic friend was talking to them or sharing his soliloquy with them.

The consequence was a copious correspondence with his readers, chiefly Americans, and women, which appears to have given Benson much pleasure. It was the pleasure, presumably, of finding that he had reached a wider audience than one made up of academics and other intellectuals, the pleasure also of feeling that, by his counsel, he had influenced lives; and, finally, the pleasure of knowing that his correspondents would not turn up in that more brisk and astringent world in which he lived.

Benson's friends were aware of his restless activity. He fancied himself an introspective man—this chiefly, it would seem, because he was neither a rigorous thinker nor an exact scholar nor an administrator. Yet he was happy only when busy; and exchanging his career as teacher at Eton for an honorary fellowship at Magdalene and a literary life was not evidence that he was introspective: he became, like his London friend Edmund Gosse, a literary man of affairs. In him, lack of firmness at center was partially concealed by firm surfaces, sociability, gossip, small duties. Always busy, he was incapable both of unabashed indolence and of 'inner working.'

Percy Lubbock delights in ironizing the opposition between the life Benson celebrated in his books and the life he actually lived. Thus, of the house he inhabited in 1906, we read: "The silent waters and solitary paths that surrounded it were all that the philosophic recluse of the House of Quiet could desire. He did not, in point of fact, desire them long. . . . His friends were not slow to admire how sociably he cultivated seclusion, how energetically he commanded repose; and he laughed when he could not gainsay them. . . ." Yet, if he could not be busy, "his spirit dropped in perplexity."

As fellow of Magdalene, Benson had status and a house to his taste but no duties save those of his own election. Yet his schedule was rigid. He spent the morning writing letters to his readers, his 'parishioners,' and to his friends (that other group); and "Nothing could persuade him to reduce this daily labor, a great part of which was purely gratuitous, required of him neither by friendship nor by duty." At one o'clock, "still writing for dear life," he was surprised by his daily luncheon party, consisting of a few Magdalene undergraduates, all of whom were bidden in turn. But the party "knew better than to linger when the hour was over"; for the afternoon must be spent in air and exercise on the road—walking or bicycling, till teatime—presumably 4, since at 4:30 he sat down to "write his chapter"—to write, at one sitting, a chapter of whatever book he then was composing. He wrote till five minutes before dinner time, when, hastily donning his gown, he went into the Hall. After dinner, wine, coffee, and conversation with the other fellows in the paneled room upstairs took another hour. And the evening ended in a game of cards with a friend, or he might "even read a little—though in general he read books only in bed, during his frequent wakeful nights. . . ."

This busy life went on, with interruptions, to the end. In 1915 Benson became master of Magdalene, one honor among those coveted which he accepted, without hesitation, probably because its duties were slight; and he was free to go on as before—writing and entertaining.

The interruptions were occasioned by two breakdowns, the latter of which was the more acute and the longer: five years. He was plunged into despair: feared not death but madness. Various methods of treatment were used: travel, idle country life, nursing homes. During his first attack (more than two years), he continued his Diary; during the second, it remained almost vacant—an ominous sign in the case of a man so addicted to self-concern and to writing.

The immediate origins and proximate terminations of these periods remained obscure. Though the cause could be officially put down to overwork, the overwork was obviously, as his friends saw, gratuitous, self-imposed. He had no talent for vacancy, idleness, or leisure. One of his candid friends wrote, "I have always thought that in this incredible speed with which he changed clothes, in this failure to draw from the recuperative resources of life, the leisurely shaving and bathing and mediation of ordinary routine, lay the seeds of Nature's slow revenge on those who are impatient of her old rhythms of energy and rest." Another, and closer, friend comments, "There was no fraction of the day in which he could relapse, like other people, into careless unperceptive ease."

In 1923 he began to recover from his last breakdown, with two years more to live, apparently his happiest. Eagerly he returned to his old routine of writing and entertaining. He produced, in but a few weeks for each, his two best volumes of reminiscence—their richness quite conceivably due to the enforced silence which preceded their composition. But he also translated epigrams from the Greek Anthology and wrote at least three novels as well as more essays. He desired to be a great writer; but that desire could not force him to the generic self-definition necessary for all save the greatest.

Benson wrote in all forms. Till forty, he was chiefly a graceful and smooth minor poet; and it was as a poet that he won his first literary name and the friendship of the once famous London critic Edmund Gosse. Then he became an 'inspirational' essayist. To his friends, Benson's "books" meant these collections of meditative essays, these lay sermons, of which the *Upton Letters* and *From a College Window* came first—these collections which they rarely looked into but viewed as the author's self-indulgences, as reflections of that soft and indolent aspect of his character which they deplored. His old friend, Reverend Dr. Lyttelton, writing for this symposium, asserts, in words to which the friends generally were willing to subscribe, that Benson's merits as the author of these books can be "summed up in this—that he wrote very charmingly, and in a very kindly spirit"; and the same clerical friend attributes the popularity of the books to the recent arrival of a new reading public which seeks a culture requiring no exertion for its attainment.

These popular books were, after a decade and more, though still selling, patronizingly reviewed, so far as reviewed at all. The reviews pained Benson, for he was incapable of profiting from any adverse criticism. (He could not revise a chapter—or a book—only discard it and write another.) But he comforted himself by reflecting he had lost not his merit but his "vogue." With equal calm, he accepted a friend's openly expressed rebuke for the disparity between his social self and his literary *persona:* "In my books, I am solemn, sweet, retired; in real life I am rather vehement, sharp, contemptuous, a busy mocker," thinking it enough to reply to these charges that he is "something of a fatalist" and that he is "really so lazy: that is my main trouble, my hurried exuberance. . . ."

If Benson's friends too often failed to distinguish among his fifty books, Benson himself could give them no help: he seems, of himself, to have made no discriminations. As a writer he entirely lacked that built-in critic of his writing every writer requires. Perhaps his relatively early success with his popular books (which he could regard as 'helpful' to others) may partly be responsible for the strange nonchalance with which he can say in his Diary, after some reading in the *Apologia*, "I wrote a little study of Newman easily and pleasantly" —a rather shocking adjective followed by yet more shocking adverbs. He will be quoted presently as thinking that what he can write "easily"—reminiscence—ought not to be as good as what he writes with more difficulty; but, after a certain age, he wrote nothing which cost him labor and pain. He was content to recognize himself as an improvisator, incapable of finishing or perfecting anything, and to leave the judgment of his improvisations to others.

His real talent was for biography, that secondary form of literature which he himself, no avid reader, chiefly read. Benson's early book on *Archbishop Laud* (written, it is said, in application for a Cambridge fellowship) is surprisingly dull for a book on so controversial a figure. As his scholarly friend Montague James observed, Benson has little or no interest in the historical setting and in the more than historic issues involved; personal details alone concern him. With his life of Archbishop Benson he succeeded much better: he was at once connected enough with his subject and detached enough from his subject's official career and objective accomplishments to write (with advisement from others) a satisfactory official biography.

But literary biography quite naturally much more engaged him. In distinguished company (including that of Henry James on Hawthorne), he wrote three volumes for the 'English Men of Letters' series, then edited by John Morley—the *Rossetti*, the *FitzGerald*, and the *Pater*, of which the last named (strangely, written in the same year as *From a College Window*) is surely the best. He showed himself perfectly capable of assembling evidence by reading accounts already in print and by interviewing survivors, of psychological and even literary commentary. And he chose, or was assigned, congenial subjects.

In 1910 and the three following years, Benson delivered at Magdalene a series of lectures devoted respectively to Ruskin, Carlyle, William Morris, and Browning, of which only the first series saw print. The *Ruskin*, subtitled *A Study in Personality*, published as read, and read evidently in a rapidly written first draft, is loose, repetitious, and sentimental. But the disparity between the *Ruskin* and the earlier biographies suggests the difference between his writing for the pleasure of it or the vague edification of others and his writing to meet the standards of an editor and of a critical friend such as Edmund Gosse, himself a contributor to the series and perhaps responsible for the invitations to Benson.

Like his friend Henry James, he savored of the past only what, partly by documents but chiefly by some personal succession, some 'laying on of hands' by a survivor, he could feel as tangible. He spoke of the only definite influence on Pater as Ruskin, whom Pater read at nineteen; and Benson wrote at the end of his life (1924) a sketch, "A Sight of Ruskin," describing how, in 1880, when he was president of a literary society of Eton boys, he met Ruskin, then sixty-one, and talked briefly with him before the lecture. From Ruskin and the Pre-Raphaelites to Henry James: that is Benson's literary time span. Literarily, he could not follow James after *The Portrait of a Lady;* but the personal, the pontifical, greatness of *der alte* James he apprehended—few better than he.

Of Rossetti, FitzGerald, and Pater, he seems never to have had a glimpse; but those who knew them intimately were still living when Benson wrote. Rich in shrewd, grotesque, but 'unslanted' detail are the pages from the 1903 diary on his Rossetti afternoon with Watts-Dunton and Swinburne; and in writing his Pater he had the assistance of Pater's two maiden-lady sisters, and Shadwell, the provost of Oriel, Pater's oldest friend, and Howard Sturgis, that Anglo-American who was the host of all literary men from James to E. M. Forster.

The *Pater* holds up, and out, remarkably well. Benson had at once to stretch and to restrain himself to write it.

In the chapter on "Early Life," Benson describes—doubtless partly to guard Pater, and perhaps himself, against any contaminating association with the celebrated artificialities of Wilde—Pater's little parlor at Brasenose, which was "always furnished with a certain seemly austerity and simplicity. . . . His only luxury was a bowl of dried rose-leaves. He had little desire to possess intrinsically valuable objects. . . ." There were a few engravings on the walls; and somewhere stood a little tray of copies of beautiful Greek coins. "His outer door was always open, he was always accessible, never seemed to be interrupted by any visitor, was never impatient, always courteous and deferential; rising . . . in the middle of the most complicated sentence. . . ."

Pater's style of writing was Pater's own invention; yet, says Benson, "it is not only easy to imitate, but it is impossible, if one studies it closely, not to fall into the very mannerisms of the writer." And Benson's book, otherwise (for him) so carefully written and so critical, would be better if it avoided that very likely unconscious imitation which, though it never essays the Pateric sentence structure, overuses certain words too dear to Pater—"blithe," "weary," "comely," "dainty," and their corresponding nouns. Yet it was, surely, a kind of discipline for him to try to sound like Pater—a writer who, despite

his delicacies, practiced always the counsel he gave his 'age':
"A *busy* age will hardly educate its writers in correctness. Let
its writers make time to write English more as a learned language."

There is another kind of biographical writing at which
Benson excelled: autobiographical writing and character
sketches—recollections of persons, commonly observed in his
youth, and rather contemporaries of his father's than his own.
The first book of this kind he published was *The Leaves of the
Tree* (1911), and of this he received praise from an acquaintance who also mentioned (but, as Benson notes, without comment) *The Silent Isle*, one of the familiar 'meditations' published at about the same time. To his Diary he confides: "It
makes me feel that this sort of reminiscence is what I can do
best. I have a close observation and a photographic eye"; he
should have added, "and a phonographic ear." But he immediately disposes of this "What I can do best" by saying, it is
"very little pleasure indeed to do it. It seems to me the sort of
thing that any one can do or ought to be able to do; I want to
criticize life, not to photograph it."

To such eminences as James and Hardy, Benson had, all
his life, easy access; and yet the charm of his portraits is partly
that it was not only the internationally, or even nationally famous, whom he delineates: he was a snob, of course, but not of
the obvious sort, the sort enamored of newspaper celebrities.
He was a connoisseur of persons, with a trained taste for many
kinds of excellence. 'People' interested him in a curiously impersonal kind of way. He was what his partial American parallel Gamaliel Bradford once called himself, a "naturalist of souls."

He was capable both of a unified characterization and
close observation and reproduction of detail. That variously
rich anthology, Simon Nowell-Smith's *Legend of the Master*
(1947), shows him to be one of the few reliable reporters of
Henry James's celebrated latter-day modes of speech and manners. The "Portrait by Arthur Benson," compounded of passages from the essay written after James's death (*Memories
and Friends*) and from the Diary, limns in not only the ges-

tures, gait, circumlocutions, and surprises, the ever-increasing adverbs, but also the tone and spirit. If we are made to see "his rolling eyes, with the heavy lines round them, his rolling resolute gait, as if he *shouldered* something and set off with his burden," we are made to feel also the combination in him of simple loyalty and emotion with intellectual complexity, the "deep impression he leaves of majesty, beauty and greatness."

Benson's richest book is *Trefoil*, ostensibly a supplement to his early, 'official' life of his father, an account of his father's prearchepiscopal labors, as headmaster of Wellington, canon of Lincoln, and first bishop of the Cornish diocese of Truro: the book is really an autobiography of Benson's own early years.

In it, there are episodes, finely told and touching, from the years in Truro—two in particular, concerning isolated Anglican priests set down among the Wesleyans. Riding with his father, bent upon episcopal visitation, he saw "an old clergyman with a long grey beard, digging in the garden, like Laertes in the *Odyssey*. . . . He asked us into a very barely furnished house . . . then bit by bit he told his story, and I shall never forget the mixture of dreariness and passionate emphasis with which he spoke. He had been 'converted,' and resolved to dedicate himself to the work of the Church. He had been ordained, and with his wife had migrated to this lonely place. He was eighty years old, and had worked there for forty years. But the place was peopled with Dissenters from the Church of England, whom he contrived to offend, and who did their best, he declared, to thwart his efforts. He had begun with a small congregation, which had dwindled to three or four persons. He knew no one in the place, had no neighbors, spoke to no one. He talked with extreme bitterness: 'I have spent my life in fighting with the beasts at Ephesus.'

"Now, he said, he only worked in the garden just to keep himself from going crazy. His wife was dead, and he had no children. He was not an attractive man at all, loud and continuous in speech, tactless and vindictive. . . . But he was deeply and horribly pathetic; and he said, when we went away, 'The

promise made to those who seek first the Kingdom of God—
for I sacrificed everything—has not been fulfilled for me.' "

Another isolated clergyman lived in a vicarage "with neither carpets nor curtains," lived on porridge and milk. The
parish was "all Dissenters. . . ." "He was evidently a good,
sensible, commonplace man, with no particular zeal or enthusiasm, very diffident and tongue-tied, and with no very pressing
message to deliver.

"My father tried to make a few suggestions, but he shook
his head; and suddenly burst into tears. Then he went on to
say that he had something much on his mind, which he felt he
must tell my father. He said, 'I am so lonely and miserable in
the evenings, that I rent a pew in the Wesleyan chapel, and go
there on Sunday nights to get a little warmth and light, and to
see human beings and hear them speak. I know it is very
wrong, but I cannot bear the perpetual solitude.' "

The central part of *Trefoil* is the account of the Cathedral, the Cathedral Close, and its denizens in the 1870's as remembered, fifty years after. Benson evaded the influence of
school and university, thinks Lubbock; it was "in the precinct
of a Cathedral that he knew himself to be truly at home. . . .
He always said that he knew the language of the minister-
world as he knew no other. . . ."

As a boy, Benson more or less took it for granted that he
would follow his father's line, advancing from the priesthood
to some higher order, presumably in the cathedral world. But
in his undergraduate years he experienced speculative doubts,
as well as some emotional crisis, both of which he put into
his fictitious and anonymous *Memoirs of Arthur Hamilton*
(1885), a book which has, for all its immaturity, a vividness
and power nowhere later to be found in his writing. Yet,
never deeply religious, he did not pass from faith to positivism.
He became what might best be called an Anglican agnostic:
not disposed to attack the Church or its doctrine but easing
the bondage of the one and softening the rigor of the other—
rather sympathetic than critical, but vague both in affirmation
and rejection.

A. C. Benson and His Friends

From his boyhood, definite theological teaching had been absent; and the "ethical element" in any overt form was also absent. His mother disliked and feared "priggishness"; his father, himself preoccupied with "moral ideas," was afraid of "scaring or boring" his children, and trusted that such ideas would be insensibly imbibed from the endless Cathedral services the family attended. Was this largely indirect training "really bracing enough"? Didn't it have an "almost dilettante effect" on young Benson? Benson opined so; his friends were certain.

As a boy, he regarded religion not as a basis of conduct but only as a "section of conduct"—charming and strange phrase which could be translated into "ritualism" if that word had not so narrowed its meaning that Anglo-Catholics are deemed "ritualistic" while Quakers are not. As a matter of sensibility, and of something more, Benson seems early to have been enamored of order—as manifest in unnamed rules and in manners and decorum. The Cathedral Close was a kind of ancient system, "a thing strangely remote from politics, social problems, sport, and even academic concerns. It was a society which might seem to an outsider to be highly artificial, but the details of which were inbibed by instinct, and so apprehended as the natural course of life. It was a big machine, the whole cathedral establishment, with a very definite subordination"—one could as well say hierarchy— "and proportion penetrating it, and knit together by an elaborate and differential kind of courtesy. . . . It was an intensely decorous and sheltered affair, but it embraced so many persons that it was an essentially good training in manners." Here Benson is, for once at least and briefly, able to generalize.

But this is at the end of a long, rich account of life in the Cathedral Close, full of detail partly architectural but chiefly personal—the two never wholly separated. Though the best examples are often too long for quoting, the qualities of quiet humor and exact observation can be illustrated by two clerical portraits.

"The Archdeacon was a small, precise-looking man, his

shoulders much bowed, bald, with a small, rather prim mouth, and with an expression strangely compounded of amiability and acuteness. He had the most courteous and deferential manner, and accompanied his remarks, which were few, cautious, and precisely phrased, with a constant succession of little bows, like a pigeon patrolling a lawn. So determined was he not to commit himself to any too definite a statement, that I remember my father saying that when a child was born to the Archdeacon, he met him in the vestry, offered his congratulations, and asked if the infant were a girl or a boy. 'I think,' said the Archdeacon, 'that I may go so far as to say that it is not a girl.' "

The Bishop of Lincoln was Christopher Wordsworth, nephew of the poet; and he and his wife, who dwelt in the Palace several miles from Lincoln, were "objects of frequent and baffled curiosity to us children." The lady's "one purpose in life was to look after the Bishop, to keep him well, to intervene between him and his tendency to entire absorption in work or thought, and to interpret him to the ordinary world. 'I suppose the Bishop is not interested in that?' said a neighboring squire to Mrs. Wordsworth. 'The Bishop is interested in everything, though I have not heard him mention that subject lately.' "

The Bishop is seen at luncheon, "utterly unaware of what he ate or drank. I can see him now . . . , wearying perhaps of the slice of mutton assigned to him, and stretching out his hand to any viands within reach—a fruit-tart, an apple, a piece of cake—and transferring it with spoon or fork to his own already occupied plate. He would take, in the intervals of his discourse, tiny morsels from the heap; then some other substance would be added, till Mrs. Wordsworth would make a sign, and the butler would remove the loaded plate and substitute a clean one—and the process would begin again. John Wordsworth [his son, afterward Bishop of Salisbury] was in respect of food one of the most absent-minded of men; but I never in all my life saw anyone so incurious as the Bishop of Lincoln—he seemed to be living in a dream."

A. C. Benson and His Friends

Trefoil is a book of much charm and, within its limits of a chiefly ecclesiastical world, much variety; it sensitively distinguishes between the wearers of clerical black. In it, there appear no really vicious, patently hypocritical, or loose-living priests; but there appear easy-living priests, priests who are primarily scholars (the Anglican Church has always been rich in such), priests who are strong, masterful men (like Benson's father, whom he more resembled than he ever knew), and even saintly and mystical priests (like Bishop Wilkinson, "the holiest man I ever saw"). In this book, Benson's own range of awareness and perception is present, arranged and composed, as nowhere else in his writings. His preeminent ocularity, his remembering eye for the detail of natural scenery and architecture, of gesture and costume, has its not inadequate balance in characterization and judgment of persons. The book has the light and warmth of Ruskin's *Praeterita*, which it most nearly recalls, but with much more of structure and continuity and a really artistic close.

One of the problems of the autobiographer—perhaps his chief, is to define his stance, his narrative point of view. Benson consciously sought to recall his story as it had presented itself to his "boyish mind and perception" and to exclude subsequent illuminations; and at that restriction he seems remarkably to have succeeded.

For checks on his accuracy, he used friends still surviving from Wellington College, Lincoln, and Truro—the three invoked pasts. For advance readers of his book and advisers on "expression and arrangement," he had (and prefatorily thanks) his brother Fred (E.F.) and his close friend, Percy Lubbock.

I I

The frequent quotations from Benson's Diary and from Lubbock have, for strategic reasons, not yet been assigned location; but they come from the same printed volume, published (though neither title page nor preface is dated) in 1926, the year after Benson's death, the year which saw also the publication of *As Seen by His Friends*.

Connections

The Diary of *Arthur Christopher Benson Arranged for Publication by Percy Lubbock* cannot be called the best of Benson's books or even the most 'interesting' (vague word for a work offering a multiplicity of attractions), but that only because it is not, in any precise sense, by Benson. It is in some sense an equivalent of the familiar genre, the 'Life and Letters,' the genre which, beginning with William Mason's *Life of Gray*, offers a man's life so far as possible in his own words, with the biographer supplying necessary factual information and continuity. Lubbock's part, however, so far exceeds that of any analogous predecessors that it seems more accurate to call the resulting book a collaboration.

Begun in 1897 and concluding only a few days before Benson's death, the Diary amounts to four million words, would compose forty substantial volumes if printed in full; while Lubbock's selection or abridgment of it comprises something like a fortieth part of the whole. The reader has therefore to trust, that the editor's choices are truly representative and not governed by some theory of the diarist's character—a large trust, but one not seriously to be questioned.

The avowed omissions are all of one sort. It was Benson's habit, after having been the delightful, the warm and charming host, self-compelled to please, and overplaying his part, to relieve himself of the discrepancy between this social role and his total judgment of his guests, his friends, by excoriating them and their behavior on paper. That this was his habit, that he set down, in such a mood, sharp things about his friends, Lubbock notes, but only as a generalization; he gives no names save his own and no examples, named or unnamed. Otherwise, we are given to understand, the selections represent, with some kind of just proportions, passages of self-analysis, characterizations of persons and places, chosen on the basis of their general interest.

Yet, granting the representativeness of the selections made, the Diary as it is in print is best regarded either as a composition by Lubbock, from whom came the structure and the proportions, the total emphasis and the tone, or as a dialogue or antiphon in which Benson and his editor, his friend, speak in turn. The commentator, clear of mind, psychologically acute, thinks that the diarist, however perceptive of others, did not understand himself; hence, that the former must correct the misapprehensions likely to be aroused by the latter.

The qualifications of Percy Lubbock for his editing of the Diary are of three sorts. He had been Benson's pupil and a member of his 'house' at Eton, and thereafter a close friend. And he, was himself a writer of stature, not 'great' but certainly distinguished—the author of two sensitive and impeccable novels and of *The Craft of Fiction* (1921), a masterly treatise on the novel, Jamesian in its assumptions, but of a strictness of doctrine in excess of James's own. Lastly, he had produced, in 1920, a collection of the *Letters of Henry James*.

Indeed, the method of the two works is the same. The selection of materials is Lubbock's; and he provides for both a substantial introductory essay, analytic and generalizing, and also a preface to each of the chapters, covering a period of years. We are offered, in effect, the biography of a literary man, illustrated by passages from his private papers, his unpublished, and personal, writings.

The method of the two works is the same; but the tone is sharply different. Lubbock admired James as a writer, a professional writer, an artist, a Master. In one of the episodes narrated in the *Diary*, James is seen, late in life and almost unsaleable, congratulating Benson on the success of his popular books—one professional congratulating another. But of course James did not really take Benson seriously *in that way*, affectionately as he valued their friendship; nor would it have occurred to Lubbock that Benson, also, was a writer, despite the fact that Benson insisted on so thinking of himself.

In an essay, "The Author of His Books," contributed to *Benson as Seen by Some Friends*, Lubbock does, temporarily, distinguish those books by kind: his popular books "hardly carry weight enough for criticism. His biographical sketches and studies are another matter. With a concrete figure before him, a human being to be represented in the appearance of life, he had a task that held his attention more firmly than any musing meditation upon a sunset in a college garden." And he does, furthermore, distinguish between Benson's good biographical studies of the famous dead and his superior portraits of men and women whom he had known, contained in his "most attractive volumes" and those which "will also prove to be his most enduring," the only volumes of his in which his friends will recognize something like the total man they knew.

And yet the final verdict, for Lubbock, has to remain that Benson was not, at center, a writer, "not *all* a writer. His books engaged him very deeply; but they only engaged, they never had possession of him." The natural medium for his talent was the spoken word; "it did not demand the written page; it could not take full advantage of it." In such wise, Lubbock defines the difference between a real writer and one who likes to write.

James was an eminent and beautiful example of the man who, without wavering, had found his vocation, been held and fortified and stayed by it. He had the immense gift of self-knowledge; while Benson, blessed in so many ways, was pathetically if not shockingly unself-knowing. Like the other friends, Lubbock avoids any word so gross as 'hypocrite'; yet he is palpably shocked that the man who writes in praise of quiet and solitude should himself seem happy only when voluble and busy; and he judges that Benson had mistaken his calling. Writing was not his work but his reward when his work was over, his between tea and dinner reward.

He should have stayed at Eton, as teacher and housemaster, perhaps have sought and accepted the headmastership. Benson had, in his friend's judgment, been a highly successful educator of a sort—a sort defined, in conscientious precision, with the aid of negatives: "a memorable master of youth,—master rather than teacher or trainer"; an "inspirer of loyalty, an awakener of admiration and devotion," but "firing enthusiasm rather than guiding or fortifying." If the praise is genuine, the reservations are serious and critical.

A. C. Benson and His Friends

Why Lubbock, holding such views of his subject, should, six years after his edition of James's *Letters*, have undertaken a similar office for Benson seems undeniably strange. Yet an answer must be found which does justice to the intellectual and moral integrity of Lubbock.

The closest analogue which presents itself is a case from Henry James's own career—his *William Wetmore Story and His Friends*, two sizable volumes published in 1903, which quite properly struck Henry Adams as a "job imposed . . . , a *tour de force*, of course. . . ." Conceal it how he will, under his latest style, with its ironies and urbanities, it is clear that James cannot take Story at his old friend's self-valuation or even self-interpretation; that he sees him as a charming and cultivated gentleman of no proper professional education who, playing at being poet, painter, and sculptor, is really a dilettante and not an artist, still less a master.

James's "job" was presumably imposed upon him by Story's survivors, his friends, and probably, it may be inferred, paid for. But, since James's artistic conscience would not let him produce a perfunctory performance, he made *Story and His Friends* into a Jamesian, half-autobiographical book, almost as much by Henry James as *A Small Boy and Others* and *Notes of a Son and Brother*.

Unlike James's view of Story, Lubbock's view of Benson is overtly expressed, which rather augments than diminishes the difficulty in accounting for the existence of the book; and no Foreword to the Diary offers explanation. Lubbock must have been invited, or commissioned, to do the work, either by Fred Benson, his brother's literary executor, or by Benson himself; and the latter seems the more probable supposition. The diarist several times, it is known, thought of destroying his Diary, yet he did not; and he may well have requested his friend to publish such parts of it as he judged worthy. A man so avid of publication, and so economical of his time as Benson, can scarcely have given his Diary so much attention without the thought of its one day seeing print; and a man so disappointed by the critical reception of his books may well have hoped that, at the last, through its medium, he, like some eminent diarists of the past, might receive serious recognition.

Lubbock, like James, had more than one loyalty to satisfy. There was the claim of his friend, "Remember me"; there was the claim of the Friends, 'Correct misapprehensions of a man we properly loved, by exhibiting the totality of him'; there was the claim of literature, 'A book should be a book and not a compilation or manufacture'; lastly, there was the claim of his own integrity. His task required, and his book evinces, the requisite combination of delicacy and firmness, of empathy and detachment.

Yet the final special richness of the *Diary* overflows and transcends Lubbock's intention. The book lingers in the memory as a dialogue rare of kind, if not indeed unique. In most titular dialogues, the Socratic included, there is but one real speaker: the other voice or voices play the subsidiary role of inquirer or foil. But, in this dialogue, securely as the voice of the student turned critical friend and spokesman for the Friends is heard, the voice of the lovable but unheroic man is heard too —the voice of the talented man of imperfect self-knowledge whose most obvious success is illicit and who arouses more stringent expectations to which he cannot rise.

The reader is of two minds, divided between sympathy and judgment, or judgment and judgment. At least, no more than the Friends can he forget Arthur Christopher Benson.

1968

Paul Elmer More

In 1909 Paul More wrote to a friend this description of his own *Shelburne Essays,* of which the Sixth Series had just been published: "The book is well calculated to miss every class of reader,—too academic for the literary, too literary for the academic, too sceptical for the religious, too religious for the sceptical; too human for the metaphysical, and too metaphysical for the human."

More well knew himself, both from self-analysis and from paying attention to how, as man and as writer, he affected others. The particular volume which prompted his generalization was subtitled, "Studies in Religious Dualism"; and it is probably not only the most unified but the best volume of the *Shelburne* series, as it is also one of the least 'literary': characteristic subjects are St. Augustine, Pascal, and Browne—literary masters who belong to the history of thought. Yet the balanced series of calculations More has set up well fits not only his *Shelburnes,* legally or loosely classified as literary criticism, but the more closely sequential volumes of 'The Greek Tradition,' the work of his later years.

When a man so ably anticipates his reviewers and other critics, what can he say in defense of his position? And, setting up and naming the polar opposites with the skill he does, how does he name the seemingly excluded middle which must be his own stance?

More never attempted to label himself. In the 1930's, when an intellectual movement somewhat analogous to the

Transcendental movement of a century before, though headed in the opposite direction, had its brief period of publicity as the 'New Humanism,' More's close friendship with the chief figure in the movement, Irving Babbitt, seemed to give him a name and a place. But More both distrusted any semblance of sectarian zeal and had himself already moved from the common ground he had shared with Babbitt to Platonism and Christian Platonism. He has been called—and can be called—a 'historian of ideas'; yet that phrase, during the period of its currency, has ever denoted the intellectual historian who, overtly at least, lacks personal commitment to any of the 'ideas' the course of which he traces—something which cannot be said of More in his 'Greek Tradition.' It would be proper to call him, in the large traditional sense, a 'humanist'; for he was a lifelong student of the Greek and Latin classics—of the Ancients—and of the Liberal Arts, those arts which (in distinction from the studies which teach a craft or a skill) shape the mind and character of a man, making him a gentleman and a philosopher, a member of the state, and a citizen of the world. And in his latter days, 'Christian humanist' would be a proper and illuminating term, associating him with such figures as Clement of Alexandria, Sir Thomas More, St. Francis of Sales, Jeremy Taylor, Sir Thomas Browne, and Baron von Hügel.

There is, however, a current and recent term which should also be invoked and applied—that of 'generalist.' The term, coined to match its antonym, 'specialist,' is unhappy—as seeming to imply that specialism is to be counteracted only by specializing in generality; but it has its use in designating those who refuse life-long confinement to their initial "field," who, starting from the particular studies of their training and profession, widen their scope of interest—either by instinct or conscious intent, their hypothetical goal being the whole range of basic and liberal knowledge, being perspective and wisdom.

Such modern transit is not limited to literary men, though literary men, and literary critics, are apt examples—as witness the cases in English and American letters, of Coleridge, Matthew Arnold, and T. S. Eliot—even of post-Eliotic 'new critics' like Tate and Blackmur, not to mention Kenneth Burke. But their examples are matched, and probably bettered, by those of William James, who began as a physiologist, and Alfred North Whitehead, who began as a mathematician, by Bertrand Russell and George Santayana, to cite men who began or ended up as philosophers, and Adams and Toynbee as historians or philosophers of history. Any man who departs from the 'field' in which he was reared, who widens his scope, is subject to adverse criticism from the professionals encamped on his few or many frontiers. This is an anticipatable charge which, after counting the risks, the convinced and responsible humanist, or generalist, will find honorable to face.

From specialist to generalist is the customary modern practice; but there are occasional examples of the archaic type —the relatively undifferentiated man possessed of the ambition to be universal—the ideal of the Renaissance man, as it has sometimes been called—the Leonardo or Milton or Goethe—the artist-scholar-philosopher, who combines action and contemplation, creation and criticism. Paul More, as one comes to see him in Arthur Dakin's scrupulously full and objective biography, seems, on whatever scale of achievement, to belong to this perhaps by now archaic type. His younger friend, T. S. Eliot, writing about him, was ignorant of the fact that More set out—so far as he had a single, all-consuming ambition—to be a major poet; but it would be more accurate to say that young More desired to become a gentleman, a scholar, an artist, a philosopher, and a saint—as well as to marry. It should be easy to make a man, even a young man, of ambitions so grandiose a figure of ridicule; and the discrepancy between such ambitions and even More's substantial achievement indicates why Alfred Kazin, discussing him at some length and with obvious interest, in *On Native Grounds*, alternates between finding him "provincial" and finding him wise and profound. The final transcendence of his ambitions and strivings, the final simplicity and grandeur of the sage or the saint he never attained—as he was aware; but it is a matter for wonder that he managed so well to surrender, in the course of a lifetime, most of his initial claims and demands, without losing his central faith in himself and, so to speak, his destiny. He never experienced a breakdown or a breakthrough, or a conversion crisis: he was always conscious of what was going on inside him: conscious at once of his zigzags and his direction.

To undertake, in the second half of the nineteenth century, to be a universal man, to begin life as a generalist, was unavoidably to commit oneself, in an age of specialization, to amateurism, of however high a level. And this, it seems to me, is what More did; and one's estimate of his achievement depends considerably on what weight one assigns to balance and centrality. Almost like the elder Henry James, rearing his sons, More, rearing himself, shrinks back from choices which represent limitation, professionalism, and expertness—whether the choice be the doctorate in Sanskrit, academic philosophy, or mysticism; his choice, chiefly shown in what he rejects, is for the human voice in its middle register, the voice of educated and refined commonsense.

There is something important to add to this account. Amateurism and generality and a high normalism: all of these are versions of the middle, of the *aurea mediocritas*. How can a man fire himself to a life of intellectual activity like More's by goals so tepid, so relaxed? The answer is that these were not, for More, *givens;* they had to be achieved. He was born not a classicist but a romanticist (whether the word be used historically or vaguely); and balance for him was achieved by opposing the thrusts of the antipodes. He was more aware than Babbitt of how 'romantic' one's revulsion from Romanticism can be; but even to the end More had to fight his romantic and sentimental tastes—which show themselves in some of the subjects he chose for his *Shelburnes* and in the personal asides and confessions in his essays and in his last books. It may well be that his "Definitions of Dualism," a rather arid and commonplace series of aphorisms published in Volume VIII of the *Shelburnes*, had an existential meaning for the author which it scarcely transmits to the reader.

And these reflections lead one to the necessary remark

that More's whole 'amateurism' and 'generalism' had behind them not the indolence of a dilettante but the force of conviction. Beneath his urbanity, More was all his life engaged in the search for truth and meaning, first of all for himself. In contrast to thinkers who start with designs for, and upon, society, More was in search of wisdom and—to use a word of yet higher intensity—'salvation.'

In his early essays on Thoreau, he twice quotes, from *Walden*, advice he took much to heart. "There are nowadays professors of philosophy but not philosophers. . . . To be a philosopher is not merely to have subtle thoughts, nor even to found a school, but so to love wisdom as to live according to its dictates a life of simplicity, independence, magnanimity, and trust. It is to solve some of the problems of life not only theoretically but practically."

II

As the foregoing reflections have suggested, More's was a complex character. To one who assumed, on the basis of their known close friendship, that he was like Irving Babbitt in temper as well as doctrine, he was, in his last years, a puzzle and a disappointment.

He appeared neither forceful preacher or lecturer, nor prophet, nor evident sage; rather, he was an urbane gentleman, somewhat, but not strikingly, handsome, always carefully and correctly dressed (for, like George Herbert, he paid proportionate attention to such matters). He had nothing picturesque or indeed signal about him, so that both his face and his voice were subsequently difficult to remember. He liked good food and wine—a cocktail before dinner, a whiskey and soda after it. His talk was easy and relaxed and well-bred, with nothing oracular or sententious about it, a little harmless and mildly witty gossip marking the absence of stiffness and pretension. If he did not seem like a prophet, he did not seem, either, like a professor, which indeed he had never really been. Nor did he seem like a writer. It would have been almost impossible to have guessed his profession except that of a gentleman—an *honnête homme,* who (in the phrase from La Rochefoucauld which Babbitt delighted to quote) "piqued himself on nothing."

But More on paper was another matter. He was able to carry on a serious dialogue by mail, his reserves and urbanities very considerably distanced by having the intercourse take place between minds rather than persons. In a period when younger literary men like T. S. Eliot were already typing their epistles, More still wrote with his pen, in a notably clear and firm hand, and in the style of a literary man or a philosopher, not an administrator. He answered his mail with astonishing promptness and punctiliousness—and not only acknowledged a letter but replied, in the manner of an earlier century, point by point to the questions raised, the problems posed. He had substantial generalizations to make—on music (for he was a competent amateur flutist), on literature, and on religion; but he also did not hesitate to point out the shortcomings, practical or intellectual, of his correspondents.

Henry James once wrote a short story, suggested to him by the double aspect of Robert Browning in later life, about the author who dined out and was an agreeable guest and talker while his inner self never left the writing table. Such a parallel would exaggerate; but certainly when More complained of being misunderstood by reviewers, of being accused of cold-bloodedness when he was a man of deep feeling and too ready tears, his reviewers and his casual acquaintances could plead that they encountered but the surface of his reserve. And it is certain that from his youth he had nourished and trained two natures—a worldly and an otherworldly, the—as he might have said—dual realities, neither of which was to be surrendered for the other, nor merged and blended with the other. He had his society and his solitude, to be balanced each against the other. This balancing of claims and the final hierarchic supremacy of the otherworldly were matters for solitary meditation and the writing of books.

It was not possible during his life for even a friend to see the whole man; and one must be grateful to Arthur Dakin for his biography of More as making accessible the pattern of More's inner or "noetic" life, the life of the mind and of the spirit. Composed chiefly of quotations from More's copious correspondence, it constitutes an equivalent for the Emersonian Journal which he did not keep and for the *Apologia pro Vita Sua*, the Newmanian history of a man's spiritual pilgrimage, which some of his friends urged More to write instead of speaking through masks and *personae*.

III

Paul Elmer More (his middle name, according to a rather common American practice, was his mother's maiden name) was born in 1864—near the end of the Civil War; and he died in 1937, before the Second World War. Like T. S. Eliot, he was a native of St. Louis, a midwestern city but a city of philosophical and musical claims and traditions; and he graduated from a liberal arts course in St. Louis' excellent Washington University before going to Harvard for graduate study. He was already a good classical scholar before leaving St. Louis, but at least equally good at the modern languages—French, Italian, Spanish, and particularly German; and then and later he read in all his languages, some of them self-acquired. During his college years he "steeped himself in German Romanticism"—the Schlegels, Tieck, Novalis: this was his private extracurricular indulgence.

Young More was a young man of tremendous ambitions, ambitions so vast as to suggest a German 'genius,' or a belated Renaissance man like Goethe, a Coleridge, or at least a Shelley, though his letters invoke none of these names: the young egotist seems to have felt in his presumable sense of uniqueness no need of parallels.

As a boy, he wrote a long poem in the style of *Endymion;* later, an uncompleted tragedy on Edwy, King of England. During a year in Europe (which followed four years of teaching at a St. Louis academy), he wrote a huge epic in which he figures as the wandering Jew. At twenty-four he wrote to his favorite sister, "I believe I shall be able to do my best work in the drama—comedy and tragedy." Meanwhile, he was student-wandering through Europe. He visited the fashionable watering place Baden-Baden, where "Music, walking, theatre, wine, and poetry sped the days like a dream." He wandered, alone, among the Alps—consumed by "morbid introspection" and "self-consuming egotism." In one Swiss village, he shut himself up in his lodging-house room, spoke to no one; let his hair grow "hideously long." He was ever susceptible to pretty girls —and restlessly in love.

In his twenties he was also absorbed in studying philosophy, reading Albertus Magnus, Scotus Erigena, and Giordano Bruno (in Latin), Spinoza, Hume, and Herbert Spencer. He had revolted against the orthodox and more or less Calvinistic Presbyterianism of his family, though, while rejecting it, to the intense distress of his mother, he was already trying out "lines of thought about religion" some of which continued the rest of his life, notably the doctrine of a God all-good but limited in power—'finite.'

The temporary outcome of his travels was a reaction from Romanticism into what More several times in later life described as "hard rationalism and materialism." A thick notebook was filled with the project of a New Philosophy which should prove once for all that the world and men are the product of a fatalistic law of chance and probability. He was to be the new Democritus, and to soar where he stumbled; he was "to accomplish what Darwin and Spencer had failed to finish." Like the epic, the potential treatise was burned, though one can plausibly conjecture the character of his rationalistic thinking by reading More's refutations of such, in his essay on Huxley, as well as elsewhere.

More had only to carry on a debate inside his own mind, to answer his own doubts and difficulties. The skeptic, the fideist, the emotional man, and the intellectual, the Epicurean, the Desert Saint, and the reconciling or partially reconciling humanist: all were inside of him.

It is difficult to summarize the murky period which followed; and it is yet more difficult to read *The Great Refusal*, a small book which More published in 1894. It is the story of a love affair, half Petrarchan and half Platonic, told partly in letters and partly in poems. It reflects both medieval mysticism and that of the Upanishads and was certainly partly suggested by the *Vita Nuova;* and the grand refusal (the celebrated titular phrase of course from Dante) is the lover's final renunciation of the Lady, in order to "dissolve in the vapors of mysticism."

The problem of a vocation was real for so variously ambitious a young man, who wanted to be a poet, a philosopher, a learned man, as well as a gentleman; since his vocation was to become, scaled down to size, some kind of harmonized version of all these ambitions, it was to learn how to gain a livelihood without any unnecessary retrenchments of living. Obviously, some kind of literary man, he could not subsist by serious writing; and, having lost his faith, he could not, like so many English writers of earlier centuries, become a clergyman: the choice was between journalism and university teaching.

He went to Harvard for three years, primarily to study Sanskrit and to take his doctorate in it; and he had as his teacher a great Orientalist who sympathized with his desire to "push beyond linguistics to an understanding of the spirit of the Vedas." Yet he decided against taking the professional degree, giving as his sufficient reason that the requisite specialized study would "occupy too large a portion of his time" and keep him from the "wide and general reading" for which he might never again have the leisure.

Two *memorabilia* of his three years at Harvard must be named. One was his almost chance coming upon a German scholarly work, Baur's *Manichäische Religionssystem,* a book which marked for him an epoch in his intellectual development—led him into the comparative study of world religions and his lifelong concern with ethical and philosophical dualism. It was the immediate stimulus of his own first published learned article, "The Influence of Hindu Thought on Manichaeism."

The other great event was his first meeting with Irving Babbitt, a year his junior, but already possessed of the massive stability of character and doctrine which he maintained until his death. Their friendship, their relationship, engages analysis. More was the more subtle, the more complex; Babbitt, simple, straightforward, unchanging. There is a touch in the contrast of temperaments reminiscent of Fénelon and Bossuet. And if Babbitt inevitably reminded his younger friends of Dr. Johnson, More had much about him of Newman—a central figure for him, at once attractive and repellent.

More had mobility, a movement around a postulated center, perhaps even the equilibrium of a dancer. Babbitt provided him a fixed *point de repère*, by reference to which he could and did judge his own position at any given time. There came an eventual 'parting of the ways,' to use Newman's phrase about his own break with Pusey and Keble; but no one has equaled the understanding and nobility of More's tribute to his old friend published at Babbitt's death.

After Harvard, More taught Greek, Latin, and Sanskrit at Bryn Mawr for two years, a respected and competent but not inspiring teacher and not much liking the education of the young. With his savings he was able to devote two further years to his own education. In the most nearly dramatic episode of his whole life, he followed, though at some distance, the example of Thoreau. He has nowhere left a detailed account of the life he lived in his weathered, red, rented, three-room cabin at Shelburne, New Hampshire, with its view to the south of Mount Moriah and to the north of a pine-covered hill; but that he chose to call his eleven volumes of critical essays the *Shelburnes* seems to indicate what a quietly momentous time of decisions this was for him. Though his life there displayed no astonishing austerity, it served the purpose expressed by the motto, in one of the Hindu tongues, inscribed upon his door: "For the sake of solitude." He read, wrote essays, translated, took the strolls gracefully sketched in "A Hermit's Notes on Thoreau," the opening piece in the first volume of the *Shelburne Essays*. One practical resolve he did make, he records in these "Notes": it was the renunciation of his epic and dramatic ambitions, the decision that "the attempt to criticize and not create literature was to be his labor in this world."

Thoreau was not the only sponsor of this experiment in defining his vocation. There were those recluses, the "Forest Philosophers of India," whose "very name," as More says in his essay on them, "shows how far they were from the lecture room"—how little they were such metaphysicians as the great Shankara, who sought to intellectualize and systematize what was for them, in More's words, "a religious and thoroughly human experience." And the memento of More's stay at Shelburne is the elegantly produced little book published in 1898, *A Century of Indian Epigrams, Chiefly from the Sanskrit of Bhartrihari*, a selection from the poems of an ancient Hindu prince who abdicated his throne, withdrew to the woods and a cavern, and there composed his meditations on the three ways of life—those of sensuous pleasure, of worldly wisdom, and of renunciation. The opening epigraph of the book is from Emerson's "Brahma"; there is an elegantly written prefatory epistle addressed to "Irving Babbitt, Esq."; and the translations well illustrate the old-fashioned, formal style of More's surviving verse.

> *Here nothing is, and nothing there,*
> *And nothing fronts me whereso'er;*
> *And reckoning all I find the whole*
> *Mere nothing, nothing—save the reckoning soul.*

> *How slow to him who haunts preferment's door*
> *The long days drag! how lightly o'er,*
> *When the awakened soul hath thrown aside*
> *Its load of worldly pride!*

> *So, lying near my cavern's rocky ledge,*
> *I'd dream at ease upon the mountain edge;*
> *And laugh a little in my heart, and then*
> *Plunge into thought again.*

The terminal line, as he acknowledges, is borrowed from a "stanza of Matthew Arnold's you were fond of quoting"—a stanza from "Obermann Once More" worth the looking up.

More did not renounce all. He was impressed by the ascetic wisdom of the Forest Philosophers; but he remembered, too, doubtless, the Hindu custom (at least till recently) that a man has first an obligation to follow a profession, marry, and raise children, before, in the second half of life, he is free to strip himself of his possessions, take his begging bowl, and devote himself to the unhampered life of the spirit.

IV

The years of wandering and experiment over, at thirty-six, More married a fine, sensible woman whom he had known since his boyhood. She bore him two daughters, and she ran the house in such a way as to keep all practical and parochial concerns from intruding upon his hours of study. In 1901 More began a series of literary editorships, including that of *The Nation*, founded after the Civil War by E. L. Godkin, and still in More's time probably the most serious and considered of American weeklies. He lived in or near New York, had an office in town, was a kind of high journalist, wrote essay-reviews (like the leading articles of the *Times Literary Supplement*), had assignments of books and reviewers to make. His own essay-reviews were written at the rate of about one a month (work which occupied his evenings at home from Monday through Friday). The best of these essay-reviews he collected as successive volumes of *Shelburne Essays*, published at the rate of about a volume a year, from 1904 till 1921. His position during these years was vaguely analogous to that of Sainte-Beuve and Edmund Wilson—that is, he earned his livelihood in a way which constituted a widely cultural education for himself.

In later life, More regretted the isolation in which he had to write his *Shelburnes*. Their quality, their seriousness both of learning and thought, the general urbanity of their style was such as to insure the publication of his books by Putnam and

Houghton, Mifflin; but they sold ill, were scantily reviewed and little read, at least by articulate readers who could give him the at once comforting and stimulating sense of an audience. In 1906 he wrote to Charles Eliot Norton (who, among his other merits, bothered to read serious younger writers and who early recognized the distinction of More, Babbitt, and Santayana): "One of the hardest things a man has to contend with here and now is his isolation. I hear so little criticism of my work that I respect. . . ."

More's critical writings belong chiefly to the period between the Victorians on the one hand (Arnold, James Russell Lowell, and Leslie Stephen) and, on the other, such 'New' critics of the 1930's as Eliot, Ransom, Wilson, Burke, Blackmur, Tate, Winters, and Leavis. The 'new' critics constitute a remarkable instance of men who have operated dialectically, who have learned from each other—indeed, a kind of 'Criticism, Incorporated.' There were distinguished critics and literary critics practicing during the 1890's and 1910's, the period of More's literary activity—such men as Chapman, Santayana, Woodberry, and Brownell; but they were all men who, like More, felt their isolation and found, through pride or indolence, no mode of collaboration. So More envied the critics of the 1930's their sense of dialogue and interplay, both with each other and with (what More lacked, and was apparently unconscious of lacking) their creative contemporaries in poetry and fiction.

More did not disregard the contemporary literature of his formative time, the 1890's and 1900's (Hearn, Lionel Johnson, the early Yeats, and Lady Gregory); but he stood in no vitalizing contact with them or with such American contemporaries as Robinson. It was his respect for T. S. Eliot and Edmund Wilson which led him, toward the end of his life, to read, and to write on, Joyce and Proust—essays of which Wilson remarks: "uncongenial to More though the subjects were, they show more grasp of what is really at issue in their books than most of the stuff which has been written to exalt them."

More's qualifications for writing literary criticism did not include a knowledge of aesthetics or literary theory. He had the disadvantages, though also the advantages, of taking the existence and nature of his subject for granted. And he did not, like some critical specialists, have a single kind of interest in literature and a single method. It is clear that he was moved by poetry, and that he responded to it aesthetically; but he lacked, what he had neither received nor devised for himself, instruments of analysis. After he quotes a poem which he admires, he can only ring English changes on the *Je ne sais quoi*, often coupling that with abstract and emotive terms: I find here, he will say, I know not what beauty, grace, grandeur. But these are at least in part 'period defects.' More did not intend, as Babbitt sometimes seems to do, to exclude the treatment of literary form and style from consideration.

His great strengths as a critic are his range, his comprehensiveness, his staying power, his not too heavily insisted upon sobriety. In the initial volumes of the series, the emphasis might be put on his range—which is from Hindu thought and literature through Greek to what occupies most, and most in detail, his attention—English and American literature from the seventeenth century into the twentieth. The titular topics of the essays are commonly single figures. But often the interest of a critic lives in the associations he makes, the contexts he provides, the sweep and diversity of his allusions; and More, who writes as a liberally educated man, has always background as well as foreground; so, though there are few essays devoted to Latin, French, German, or Italian authors, the critic often refers to them and their literatures, sometimes at length.

More is not an incisive, still less a brilliant critic. He has none of the bravura of Lowell, who, in penalty, is rarely coherent intellectually throughout the length of an essay, but now copies out his scholarly marginalia, now turns on his showy satire, now ends with some rather perfunctory ethical commonplace. More rarely wearies; rarely excites; does not lend himself to representation in anthologies. His moral and intellectual discipline, his information and his meditations upon it, are steadily present. From time to time in his essays, there is

an extended passage given to tracing the history of some doctrine or trend—in effect, an excursion into the 'history of
ideas'; but these almost always appear in connection with some
person, some author—providing the background for what is intended to be a balanced and "rounded" estimate of the writer.

If ethics is one, perhaps the dominant, interest of the
Shelburnes, it often takes the form of 'case history,' that is, analyzed biography. To More, in retrospect, his literary criticism
seemed a reaction against metaphysics, prompted by "a deep-
seated interest in humanity" and pursued in particular by the
exploration of human souls. He read widely in journals and
letters (subsidiary forms of literature) expecting, or at least
hoping, to discover the secrets of the human heart and to learn
how to live—the method and the art of happiness. Like Sainte-
Beuve and Matthew Arnold, he often wrote of minor figures
in whom the personality was more significant than the art. He
had essays on Cowper's letters and Lady Wortley Montagu's
and Gray's; essays on Swift's Journals and Fanny Burney's; essays on Charles Lamb and his Friends. To the end of his life he
still found much of his entertainment in reading a good leisurely nineteenth-century biography like the four-volume Life
and Letters of Dr. Pusey.

But he gave up expecting to learn, from biography, the
art of living—by which he meant the achievement of a life satisfactory in all its parts, including an old age which was a real
maturity, which had arrived at a real wisdom; for most men,
he found, had a long struggle to reach the height of their powers and find their place; then a brief plateau of success and recognition; then a decline, if not into obscurity, at least into the
inner failure of disillusionment and bitterness.

Among the major literary genres, More's preference was
clearly for poetry (under which he included drama). Though
he was well-read in the novel (Dickens, Thackeray, Meredith,
Gissing, Hawthorne, Trollope—on the last three of which, his
favorites, he wrote well) he seems to have retained much of
the old-fashioned Puritan sense that novels are not quite serious
literature—a judgment based upon the assumption that novels

deal with manners—the shifting and the phenomenological, while poetry (under which he could doubtless subsume such romances as *The Scarlet Letter* and *John Inglesant*) concerns the unchanging, those ethical insights which make poetry more philosophical than history.

More took American literature in his stride: was remarkably unprovincial in his treatment of it; saw it as a part of world literature, neither exalting it beyond its comparative weight, nor minimizing its importance for Americans as our particularly usable past. The center of our national literature was for him naturally the literature of New England, especially Emerson, Thoreau, Hawthorne, and Whittier; but his essays on Poe and Whitman are intelligent, and balanced between censure and praise. Lowell, who seems in some of his essays the archetype of the New Humanist, is, if one stops to think about it, conspicuously absent from treatment; and More's sympathetic essays on Thoreau evince not even awareness of Lowell's supercilious dismissal. There is fine historical imagination in More's studies of the Puritan and the Gothic elements in our literary tradition.

It was at one time the fashion to represent More as some kind of latter-day Puritan; but he was almost as critical as Arnold of Hebraism without Hellenism, and warningly pointed out that the New England Puritans represented but a faction of English culture: "They did not bring with them the full temper of the English people, or even that part of its character which has given us Chaucer and Shakespeare and Dryden and Swift and Johnson and Byron and Tennyson."

More was increasingly drawn to English literature of the seventeenth and eighteenth centuries. The unworldly and congenitally Platonic part of him was drawn to the 'metaphysical' poets, the Cambridge Platonists, and the Golden Age of the Anglican Church (the theologians of which became his later companions). The man of the world in him enabled him to write, in *With the Wits*, the praise of satire and some spirited illuminations of Swift, Pope, Halifax, and Chesterfield. Of Chesterfield he remarked, "his instruction . . . is not so shocking to me as perhaps it ought to be." "Love, or gallantry if you choose, was to Chesterfield only a chapter in the larger art of living." The "ages when life has seemed most noble and beautiful have commonly accepted this *ars amandi* as a necessary part of their code"; and a denial of the code "has too often meant . . . a retention of their vice with a loss of their grace."

But neither the Elizabethan nor the neoclassical period quite satisfied him—the one, rich but loose of form; the other, too thinly formal, too rationalistic. When he considered French literature, he found in its Classical period (in the abstract, at least) the requisite synthesis of this world and the other, of passion and judgment, never quite at once given in the literature of England.

Unlike the books of Arnold and Eliot, which divide rather neatly into works of literary criticism and extra-literary works on society, religion, and education, More's collections, from their start, included, along with essays on authors, some on political and social topics; but the ninth volume, *Aristocracy and Justice* (as in Plato, the two are found compatible), is entirely devoted to the defense of traditional classical education and the related concept of 'natural aristocracy'—the phrase borrowed from John Adams, the general principles, from Edmund Burke. This is not its author's strongest book; More's conservatism is of an old-fashioned and unreformed variety. He does not distinguish between private property in its strict Distributist sense and 'finance-capitalism'; nor adequately differentiate aristocracy from plutocracy. But the book is not stupid or to be regretted. Without it, More's 'generalism' would be incomplete.

Two of the *Shelburne* essays discuss critics and their function. The one given to Sainte-Beuve significantly contrasts with Babbitt's treatment of the same in *Masters of French Criticism*. Both men, with reservations, admired the great Universal Doctor of the nineteenth century; but Babbitt is impersonal in his discussion, while More (in the midst of making a career for himself as a critic) is always thinking of his own case as he writes, always making perceptible acts of identification or withdrawal of identification.

By the high claims he made for his profession in "Criticism," More somewhat reminds one of the poets writing in defense of poetry. Arnold, he says, "belongs to one of the great families of human intelligence, which begins with Cicero, the father of them all, and passes through Erasmus and Boileau and Shaftesbury and Sainte-Beuve." He contrasts the critics (who "deal much" with the criticism of literature because in literature, most manifestly, life "displays its infinitely varied motives and results" but are not restricted to literature) with two other types of intelligence—"creative writers, so-called" and "the great fulminators of new creeds" who found religions and political parties; and, while he deplores "such a timid search for the whole truth as paralyzes the will" and grants the superior efficiency of the man of one idea over the man of critical temper, he not only prefers the critical minds to those of men like Rousseau, Luther, and St. Paul, but wonders whether finally Cicero has not had "as dynamic an influence" as St. Paul. He asserts that, at a certain point, "criticism becomes almost identical with education"; and, in a very bold and striking passage, recalling the Gnostic doctrine of the Logos and half anticipating Proust, he declares that the "larger memory . . . may not unmeaningly be regarded as the purpose of activity, and literature may not too presumptuously be cherished as the final end of existence."

v

In 1914, when he was fifty, More resigned the editorship of *The Nation,* which had shifted ownership with a consequent shift in politics to the left of center. His wife's inheritance, shortly before, of a sizable estate freed him from the necessity of finding an equivalent post and livelihood. The family moved from New York to Princeton; and thereafter, though with part-time attachments to the University as lecturer first in philosophy and then in Greek, More was endowed with leisure for his own pursuits. In an unsigned parting editorial for *The Nation,* he evoked "The Air of Quiet Study" which he anticipated breathing. He praised the gradually disappearing life of the independent scholar "whose library is to him a university," the "old idea of the gentleman and scholar, as exemplified in Gibbon and a host of great names," the "joy of an intellectual purpose steadily followed, year after year, binding day to day in orderly interest, and leaving no approach to the ravaging attacks of *ennui*." The mood of this essay is continued in one of his finest appreciative essays, the Introduction to Gissing's *Private Papers of Henry Ryecroft,* written for 1918 publication in the newly founded 'Modern Library.'

Some secluded scholars have, like Thomas Gray (whose 'white melancholy' interested More as it had Arnold before him) passed their days in the harmless but purposeless acquisition of miscellaneous knowledge. More was not such a man. When he was master of his own time and free to undertake some large-scale and systematic intellectual work, he had such a project already in mind; and he established an order for his day, mostly of reading and writing, which commonly began with some Greek (Plato or the Eastern Church Fathers) and was followed by two or three hours of writing on the book upon which he was engaged.

Even in Arcadian Princeton, he felt spiritually isolated; for, as Edmund Wilson, who has graphically described a call upon him, says, he stood out against the background of University professors "not merely through his distinction of learning, his Greek and Sanskrit and Hebrew and Persian and the rest, but by virtue of his unremitting seriousness, his stubborn insistence on the importance of maintaining in one's relation to literature a position which should be realistic in the sense that it would never lose contact with moral problems as he himself understood them. . . ."

The substantial work of More's later years was *The Greek Tradition: From the Death of Socrates to the Council of Chalcedon* (399 B.C. to 451 A.D.), in four volumes, with two "complementary volumes," *Platonism,* first published in 1917, and *The Catholic Faith*, published in 1931. In these books More is no longer a literary critic; he is a philosopher—or rather, perhaps, a historian of philosophy as philosophy passes into theology; he is akin in temper to the Christian Platonists of Alexandria and still more to the Cambridge Platonists of the English seventeenth century.

More's concern with Plato had been of long standing. In 1898, the year when he published his *Century of Indian Epigrams*, he published also another small book, entitled *The Judgment of Socrates*, containing, after an introductory essay on Socrates, his own translations of the *Apology*, the *Crito*, and the closing scene of the *Phaedo*. During the earlier volumes of the *Shelburnes*, one can trace the gradual disappearance of terms and concepts from the Vedanta philosophy and the gradual triumph of the alternative great idealistic system and world-view of the Near East and the West, Platonism, even though sometimes the distinctions between the phenomenal world and the real, between appearance and reality, or illusion and reality, or the changing and the permanent have linguistic tones which blend the two traditions.

The Eighth Series of *Shelburnes* contains More's first attempt at expressing his own philosophical position in ninety "Definitions of Dualism," of which the ninetieth begins: "Self-recollection is the quiet and deliberate gathering of the mind from the many to the One. Prayer is the same act directed to the One imagined as the infinite, Eternal God" and ends with the praise of "that religious philosophy which has been called the *amor dei intellectualis*. . . ." When he came to write *Platonism* he referred to these "Definitions" as themselves the result of his study of the *Dialogues* of Plato; and he expressly rejected "any pretense to originality."

The 1917 Preface to *Platonism* is a modest and lucid statement of More's design. For him "the ethical theme" is "certainly the mainspring of [Plato's] philosophy"; and indeed throughout More's work the epistemological and metaphysical aspects of Plato's never finally systematized thought are minimized or dismissed as unprofitable and speculative. What is valuable in Plato for him is identifiably Socratic—concerned with the understanding of man (as distinct from nature and scientific knowledge), the understanding of man and the ethical law for man—the voice of the *daemon* (equated by More with conscience), and the pursuit of self-knowledge, the renunciation of sophistry and appeals to external powers, whether those of the masses or other tyrants.

My intent, More goes on to say, is not, either in this volume or its sequels, primarily to "produce a work of history," even though historical accuracy must be the necessary preliminary. It is, rather, "to write what a Greek Platonist would have called a *Protrepticus*, an invitation . . . to the practice of philosophy"—an invitation especially addressed to young college men who find "the intellectual life [as practiced today] deprived of centre or significance. . . . Only through the centralizing force of religious faith or *through its equivalent* in philosophy can the intellectual life regain its meaning and authority for earnest men."

Partially comparable instances come to mind—Newman's for one, and Brownson's for another—of men who have converted themselves in the process of writing. For More wrote *Platonism* while still a philosopher; and before the end of *The Greek Tradition* he found himself a Christian and an Anglican. To the Episcopal Church as offering a liturgical mode of worship, More had been attracted in his days as a New York editor, when he was still creedless and vaguely religious. Now he found himself gradually being converted from religiosity to belief, finding in the Incarnation the fulfillment of the Platonic hope and in the Eucharist a center for incarnational worship. His was a kind of seventeenth-century Anglicanism brought up to date. The true Church must be a *via media* between the extremes of Protestant individualism and laxity and Roman Catholic rigidity; the Church must, in his terms, be authoritarian without being absolutist. In the terms of an Anglican manifesto of 1926, it must be "Catholic *and* Critical."

It is characteristic of More that he arrived at his Catholic Faith on Protestant principles—that is, instead of making a single act of assenting faith, he proceeded to bear his critical weight upon each dogma and practice in turn. Thus, though he was able, in some sense, to affirm his belief in each article of the Apostles' Creed, he took it upon himself to decide which should be taken literally and which symbolically.

The comprehensive Anglican Church was grateful for More's adhesion, ready to administer the rite of Confirmation and receive him into her Communion; but, despite repeated invitations from his friend, the Bishop of New Jersey, More allowed scruples and hesitations to deter acceptance till, as his end neared, he decided to die as he had so long lived, in the anteroom of the Church, in the Porch of the Temple. And he died, leaving for posthumous publication, his little spiritual testament, *Pages from an Oxford Diary*, the touchingly told story of his pilgrimage in search of wisdom and salvation, a search rewarded by approximate peace.

Shortly before his friend's death, T. S. Eliot wrote these carefully considered words, expressly about *The Greek Tradition*, which Eliot judged to be More's greatest work, but susceptible of application to all his writings: "What will keep his work permanently alive . . . is that nowhere is it a mere exercise of intellect, intelligence, and erudition, or the mere demonstration of a thesis held by the mind. . . . More's works are, in the deepest sense, his autobiography. One is always aware of the sincerity, and in the later works the Christian humility, of the concentrated mind seeking God. . . ." This is finely and justly said; so too, and in a lower key, is the testimony of his almost self-effacing intelligent biographer, A. H. Dakin: More's books, "which first made him partially known, may themselves be better understood as expressions . . . of a character memorable for a high degree of frankness, wisdom, and integrity. The record of such a man . . . grappling with serious artistic, ethical, philosophical and religious subjects . . . may provoke and reward thought even in those least congenial to his temperament, methods, and conclusions."

These two statements are both bold and cautious, and in being so are tributes to the character of a man and writer ambitious of scope and almost unduly modest in his estimates of his achievement. Such an amateur, such a generalist, such a seeker after wisdom has left no completed system of thought, no single impeccable and imperishable book. It is his distinction to represent the principles which are naturally so little insisted on by men of specialized genius—that civilization is a corporate achievement, that orthodoxy is a *consensus gentium*, that society is held together by the presence in it of men of general parts and powers, of intelligence and good will, that—more important than any improvement of instrumentalities and agencies—is the critical contemplation of ends.

1969

Continuity and Coherence in the Criticism of T. S. Eliot

There would be general consent among serious readers of Anglo-American poetry and criticism, I suppose, that T. S. Eliot
has already become a classic of poetry and criticism and that
subsequent 'improvements' are unlikely to dislodge him from
that position. His rank in contemporary poetry is with Yeats.
In criticism, his status is quite as isolate.

In common practice, critical reflection succeeds to creative exercise; but the poet and the critic in Eliot began almost
concurrently (*Prufrock and Other Observations*, 1917; *The
Sacred Wood*, 1920) and have coexisted in close relation. In the
poetry there has always been implicit a criticism of life; but,
more, the poetry has been itself the fastidious product of a
critical mind, impatient with the first thought and the loosely
approximate phrase. The criticism, in turn, has been chiefly
criticism of poetry, dramatic, epic, and meditative—most of
this is recognizable (like Coleridge's and unlike Arnold's) as
the work of a poet analyzing for the benefit of his own art the
achievements of others and addressed at the general reader
only through the form of a poet's counsel to poets—ultimately,
to himself. Thus, Eliot's long—and, for him, specialized—study
of the Elizabethans was evidently sustained by his desire to re-
vive poetic drama, a desire which much later found expression
in *Murder in the Cathedral, Family Reunion,* and *The Cocktail Party;* his interest in the past of English poetry has never

been antiquarian or merely historical: he has been in search of a past which contemporary poetry—more specifically, his own —could turn to account.

This double resonance of poet and critic has given Eliot's name its authority, its place in the roll of English literary dictators which begins with Ben Jonson, follows with Dryden, Pope, and Samuel Johnson (upon whose poetry Eliot has written an admirable essay), and carries through the nineteenth century with the careers of those poet-critic-theologians, Coleridge and Arnold.

Eliot is not an easy critic to summarize or outline. Trained in Oriental and Occidental philosophy, he has learned from his teachers rather caution than system-building. Prose like that of *The Idea of a Christian Society* is almost infuriating by virtue of the things which, amid a hundred implications and qualifications, it leaves unsaid. Perhaps the chief of his 'teachers' in this cautious and elegant precision is the British neo-Hegelian, F. H. Bradley, on whom Eliot wrote a Harvard dissertation. *Selected Essays* commemorates Bradley in a brilliant piece written in 1926 upon the republication of the philosopher's *Ethical Studies*.

Since his conversion to Anglo-Catholicism some time in the 1920's, readers have inquired and wondered concerning Eliot's grounds for faith in a time of which one might say, as the great eighteenth-century Anglican Bishop Joseph Butler did of his own, "It is come . . . to be taken for granted by many persons that Christianity is not so much a subject of inquiry, but that it is now at length discovered to be fictitious." But Eliot has produced no apologia for his conversion; nor has he attempted to argue his political philosophy, which appears to be the Distributism of Chesterton and Belloc, best expressed in Belloc's *The Servile State*. He once described himself—in a statement which he has since regretted for its pontificality—as Anglo-Catholic in religion, royalist in politics, and classicist in literature; but he has long ago repented, not of his allegiances, but of his tone. His literary creed he is ready to defend; but, in spite of an increasing shift of interest from poetry and aesthetic analysis to sociology and theology, he has the full modern respect for specialized expertness and is unwilling to make the case for political or theological truth rest upon such arguments as a mere literary man can provide. In notes and appendices, he will refer to his political and theological experts; but he shrinks in dismay from such frontal invasions as Arnold made in *Literature and Dogma*.

He has repeatedly repudiated two positions characteristic of the nineteenth century and specifically of the criticism of Arnold: (1) that the poet possesses some special insight into the nature of reality, and (2) that poetry will more and more take the place of religion. He wrote in 1927, "I can see no reason for believing that either Dante or Shakespeare did any thinking on his own. . . . The difference between Shakespeare and Dante is that Dante had one coherent system of thought behind him. . . . The poet who 'thinks' is merely the poet who can express the emotional equivalent of thought." The business of the poet is to produce "objective correlatives" for thought, the imaginative illusion of a view of life. Of the nineteenth century and the Arnoldian belief in "salvation by poetry," Eliot declares, "The decay of religion, and the attrition of political institutions, left dubious frontiers upon which the poet encroached; and the annexations of the poet were legitimized by the critics. For a long time the poet is the priest; there are still, I believe, people who imagine that they draw religious aliment from Browning or Meredith."

Despite his pontifical style, of which he is aware, Eliot is not only a shy and self-distrustful but a spiritually humble man. Of the poet's work he says, "We shall often find that not only the best, but the most individual parts of his work may be those in which the dead poets, his ancestors, assert their immortality most vigorously"; and, discussing the function of criticism, he writes, "Those of us who find ourselves supporting . . . classicism believe that men cannot get on without giving allegiance to something outside themselves." As in poetry, he has been unembarrassed by indicating his teachers—Dante, Webster, Donne, Dryden, Laforgue, Corbière, Pound,—so in criticism, extrinsic and intrinsic, he has confessed his debts—confessions which must not be negated because they are often accompanied by that kind of detailed dissent which, when he comes of age, a grateful student must always make from the tenets of his teacher. When the full chronicle of Eliot's tutelage comes to be written, the parts played in the formation of his mind by Arnold, by F. H. Bradley, by Remy de Gourmont, by T. E. Hulme, by Ezra Pound, and by Irving Babbitt will be made clear.

His Harvard teacher he has called "one of the most remarkable of our critics, one who is fundamentally on most questions in the right, and very often right alone . . ."; and at the time of the Humanist controversy, when Eliot, already convinced that only the Catholic Church could save civilization, was most remote from his affectionate allegiance, he could write, "Having myself begun as a disciple of Mr. Babbitt, I feel that I have rejected nothing that seems to me positive in his teaching. . . ." The influence of Babbitt has, in important respects, grown stronger in recent years.

One must remember that Eliot has a less dogmatic but a more subtle mind than that of his teacher, and, further, that Eliot is and was a poet, while Babbitt was markedly insensitive to the arts except as the media of propaganda. Eliot, too, felt that Babbitt was—what perhaps followed from his lack of sensibility—inadequately aware of how, concretely, civilization is transmitted, through tradition, ritual, manners, and etiquette. In "his interest in the messages of individuals—messages conveyed in books—he has tended" says Eliot, "to neglect the conditions. The great men whom he holds up for our admiration and example are torn from their contexts of race, place, and time." Eliot must make a two-fold translation: as a man, he must find an 'objective correlative,' an institution, an organism which should supply the continuum and the incarnation for the sporadic abstraction, humanism; and as a poet, he must discover the aesthetic equivalent of what was represented by Babbitt chiefly as a matter of sound ethical insight—classicism.

The first of these needs led Eliot to England—where

Henry James had found civilization still extant—and the Anglican Church, and later to Agrarian Distributism, upon which, as represented by Southerners, Ransom, Tate, and Davidson, he bestowed his apostolic blessing. The second took earliest expression in the famous essay of 1917 "Tradition and the Individual Talent," in many respects the germinal essay of Eliot's whole thought.

Babbitt had indoctrinated the young poet with his own anti-Romantic bias; and "Tradition and the Individual Talent" can best be understood as an artist's version of *Rousseau and Romanticism*. Babbitt had derisively reiterated Rousseau's "I may not be better than other men, but I am at least different"; and Eliot repudiates, with all the zeal of a convert, any ambition to 'difference.' "The artist's concern with originality . . . may be considered as largely negative: he wishes only to avoid saying what has already been said as well as it can be. . . . To assert that a work is 'original' should be very modest praise: it should be no more than to say that the work is not patently negligible."

The quotations just made come from a work written in 1934; and *After Strange Gods* returns in a fashion to the essay of 1917, "Tradition and the Individual Talent," to which the older author prefatorily adverts, "I do not repudiate what I wrote in that essay any more fully than I should expect to do after such a long lapse of time. The problem, naturally, does not seem to me so simple as it seemed then, nor could I treat it now as a purely literary one."

The "purely literary" treatment of 1917 might be rehearsed something as follows. Babbitt had talked of philosophical and moral tradition; Eliot, meditating the office of the poet, and concerned, then, neither to affirm nor to deny the transmission of ideology, translated what he apprehended into a parallel doctrine of aesthetic continuity. He was impressed by what Babbitt had to reiterate concerning the difference between the Renaissance conception of the poet as a man of learning and of literary craft (a technical discipline) and the Romantic conception of the poet as a child, a dreamer, and a prophet, whose spontaneity was the badge of his office, whose poems were personal confessions, and whose production was unlikely to survive the adolescent years of eager curiosity concerning the self, eager contemplation of first love.

Eliot wanted to discover the power of self-renewal. Why, in particular, was the history of American poetry so replete with unfulfilled promise? Was it not that, in too narrow and literal a sense, the poet "looked into *his heart* and wrote?" Eliot was asking these questions of himself first of all; for he wrote the essay as he was nearing thirty, five years before the publication of *The Waste Land,* his first attempt at sustained poetry.

Answering his own questions in a "purely literary" way, he had to reply that the poet can and must draw upon a strength outside himself, that of his ancestral poets, that of the communion of poets. The "historical sense . . . we may call nearly indispensable to any one who would continue to be a poet beyond his twenty-fifth year; and the historical sense involves a perception, not only of the pastness of the past, but of its presence; the historical sense compels a man to write not merely with his own generation in his bones, but with a feeling that the whole of the *literature of Europe* from Homer and within it the whole of the literature of his own country has a simultaneous existence and composes a simultaneous order."

Like Babbitt, Eliot has always been concerned not with the historical scholar's or the Romanticist's "pastness of the past" but with the classicist's and critic's and poet's "awareness of the presence of the past." Science improves, but art—except with specific modes—does not; and Eliot has never had the modernist's patronizing pity for the dead masters or Dr. Johnson's regret for Milton, who wrote before Waller and Denham had refined our numbers.

As the poet's learning is a realization, not a discovery of new facts about the facts, so it is by no means necessarily a matter of courses and degrees. "Some can absorb knowledge; the more tardy must sweat for it." The neoclassical inquiry concerning Shakespeare's learning is essentially academic, for "Shakespeare acquired more essential history from Plutarch than most men could from the whole British Museum."

The corollary of this antiromantic attachment to tradition and the "presence of the past" is Eliot's attack on what C. S. Lewis has termed the "Personal Heresy" and what may more obviously be described as the biographical approach to literature.

"Honest criticism and sensitive appreciation are directed not upon the poet but upon the poetry." The test of a poet's achievement is that he has given self-subsistent life to a poem, that it can be understood and valued without referentially attaching itself to the biography of its author. And this counsel applies to the poet as well as the reader, for the good poet is not concerned to perpetuate his private self. "Poetry is not a turning loose of emotion, but an escape from emotion; it is not the expression of personality, but an escape from personality."

All this sounds like a kind of classicism, and Eliot has several times named himself of that fold. But, still less than Babbitt's, is his classicism to be identified with "Be Homer's works your study and delight." Eliot has, to be sure, an affection for neoclassical artists like Ben Jonson (of whom he has written with penetration and justice), as well as for Dryden, Pope, Johnson, and Racine; but his 'classicism' includes, in some sense, also Dante, Villon, and Baudelaire.

After Strange Gods does not succeed in making wholly clear what 'classicism' means to Eliot: The terms which stand for our basic concepts, the concepts *through which* we think, are exactly the terms we have most difficulty in defining; but he offers two suggestive elucidations. Speaking as a poet who had produced poetry which seemed to Babbitt and Paul More (as well as to Yvor Winters) anything but classical, Eliot makes the shrewd point that "romanticism and classicism are not matters with which *creative writers* can afford to bother overmuch; . . . I doubt whether any poet has ever done himself anything but harm by attempting to write as a 'romanticist' or as a 'classicist.' No sensible author, in the midst of something that he is trying to write, can stop to consider whether it is going to be romantic or the opposite." "*At the moment when one* writes, one is what one is, and the damage of a lifetime, and of having been born into an unsettled society, cannot be repaired at the moment of composition."

The second elucidation is offered by the word 'society.' "Tradition" is not a purely literary term. It plays an important part in Catholic theology; and families and countries have their traditions. As he passes from the literary to the extraliterary, Eliot enlarges without substantially altering his sense of tradition, associating it with "orthodoxy," as the lack of tradition is to be associated with heterodoxy or heresy. Tradition "is not solely or primarily the maintenance of dogmatic beliefs; . . . it involves all those habitual actions, habits, and customs . . . which represent the blood kinship of 'the same people living in the same place,' " the mores of a homogeneous population; it is "a way of feeling and acting," largely unconscious, whereas its correlative, orthodoxy, is "a matter which calls for the exercise of all our conscious intelligence." Tradition "has not the means to criticize itself"; and hence the need of a living orthodoxy, expressing itself in philosophy of religion as well as dogma, and maintained (Eliot has suggested, in language suggestive of Coleridge's) by a "clerisy" of Christian intellectuals.

Unlike Babbitt, Eliot still makes a distinction between *literary* criticism and *moral*. Of *After Strange Gods*, he says, "I ascended the platform . . . only in the role of moralist," though to be sure he draws illustrations of morality and immorality from works of literature. Like Babbitt, Eliot knows that art and prudence belong together in life; but, like Aristotle and Maritain, Eliot believes that it promotes confusion not to allow for and to practice a preliminary distinction between Poetics, Ethics, and Politics.

To return to Eliot's literary criticism: After "Tradition," his most famous and perhaps even more influential essay is that on the "Metaphysical Poets," published in 1921. This essay inaugurated a new hierarchic pattern for the history of English poetry. "From time to time, every hundred years or so, it is desirable that some critic shall appear to review the past of our literature, and set the poets and the poems in a new order. . . . Dryden, Johnson, and Arnold have each performed the task as well as human frailty will allow. The majority of critics can be expected only to parrot the opinions of the last master of criticism; among more independent minds a period of destruction, of preposterous over-estimation, and of successive fashions takes place, until a new authority comes to introduce some order."

Eliot modestly desists from naming himself as, in this important capacity, Arnold's successor; but the Harvard audience of 1933 who listened to the first series of Norton Lectures could readily supply the name. This evaluation, which has been systematized and popularized by F. R. Leavis and Cleanth Brooks, extends through the range of Eliot's essays on English poetry and drama, but is most concentratedly offered in his review of Grierson's *Metaphysical Lyrics*. Arnold, in his "Study of Poetry," had rushed from the Elizabethans, whose quality we are supposed to know and esteem, to the ethical Wordsworth. There was the inadequately serious Chaucer, then Shakespeare, "free" from the necessity of abiding our question; then—after a sad interregnum of neoclassical verse, which lacked more than the virtues of prose, and of Gray, a frail classic, and of Burns, with his triple Scotch—'At last, Wordsworth came.'

For Eliot, the height of English poetry comes earlier—in the late Elizabethans, the Jacobeans, and the Carolines. "The language went on and in some respects improved; the best verse of Collins, Gray, Johnson, and even Goldsmith satisfies some of our fastidious demands better than that of Donne or Marvell or King. But while the language became more refined, the feeling grew more crude."

Eliot's theory of poetry falls neither into didacticism nor into the opposite heresies of imagism and echolalia. The real 'purity' of poetry—to speak in terms at once paradoxical and generic—is to be constantly and richly impure: neither philosophy, nor psychology, nor imagery, nor music alone but a significant compounding of them all.

Orthodoxy is always more difficult to state than heresy, which is the development of an isolated 'truth'; but Eliot excels at copious illustration and analysis of illustration; and his conception of poetic orthodoxy and the hierarchy of poets which he has arranged according to it may be said to have supplanted Arnold's.

This brilliantly sensitive analysis of illustrations cannot be exhibited by excerpts. And, accurate as one trusts one's statements of Eliot's general position to be, one who places him, as I do, in the first rank of all critics past and present, must feel that schematic outlines do him a special injustice. His characteristic virtue lies less in perspective than in that close study of the poetic text of which he was, in English, the inaugurator, and in the extraordinary kind of critical wit by which he compares, by virtue of a special, shared quality or category, historically and sometimes stylistically dissimilar poets—for example, Mallarmé and Dryden.

The critical instruments he once named as chief—analysis and comparison—he has used with exemplary skill. If his interest has gradually shifted from intrinsic criticism, it has been a shift of emphasis rather than a repudiation. The total effect of consecutively rereading Eliot's remarkable criticism—written over a considerable time, and chiefly 'occasional'—is to be surprised far less by disjunction than by continuity and development.

[written *1940*]

II

The conversion of Eliot to Christianity, and specifically Anglicanism, did not interrupt the continuity of his work either in criticism or in poetry. But it did introduce a new element, or concretize an old one, which required time for appropriation and assimilation.

It would be impossible to date Eliot's 'conversion'—certainly, as with other men of his reflective and inward nature, a gradual and long continued thing. In his case, the conversion took at the least ten years, for in 1917 he was publishing reviews of books by such distinguished British philosophers of religion as Arthur Balfour, Professor Clement Webb, and Bishop William Temple which show knowledge and sympathy, as well as doubts and reserves: the tenets of the 'personality' of God and of 'personal immortality' were for him particular difficulties, to be contrasted (as in the thinking of Babbitt and the earlier More) with the purer spirituality of Hinduism and especially Hinayana Buddhism. (All his life, Eliot was to remain aware, as most men and most Christians are not, of systems of religion and culture outside of the Western alternatives.)

In "To Criticize the Critic," for him a remarkably overt piece of autobiography, Eliot tells us not how or when he was converted but when—in 1927, and as an honest obligation to a revered Master, Irving Babbitt—he announced his recent baptism and his confirmation into the English Church. He tells us, too, that it was Babbitt's immediate challenge, "I think you should come out into the open," which prompted him to preface *For Lancelot Andrewes* (1928) with the declaration that he was a classicist, a royalist, and an Anglo-Catholic.

It was no skillful and potent personal influence which effected Eliot's conversion either to religion, or to the Christian, the Anglican, and the Anglo-Catholic version of it. In 1937, attempting to define what the subsequent friendship with Paul Elmer More meant, Eliot wrote: "The English Church was familiar with the backslider, but it knew nothing of the convert —certainly not of the convert who had come such a long journey. I might almost say that I never met any Christian until after I had made up my mind to become one." Like Donne, Newman, and Orestes Brownson, Eliot converted himself—by reading and thinking.

Probably Pascal's *Pensées* was, more than any other single book, the instrument of the conversion; certainly the introduction to the *Thoughts* which Eliot wrote for 'Everyman's Library' (1931) remains not only the finest single religious essay he ever wrote but the nearest to that statement which (for whatever reasons) he was never willing to offer of his 'grounds' for the adoption of an intellectual position distancing him from so many former allies. Pascal's Jansenism was not likely to deter the austere Eliot, who defines Jansenism as "morally a Puritan movement within the Church," with "standards of conduct . . . at least as severe as those of any Puritanism in England or America"; nor was Pascal's acquaintance with "fashionable society," which precluded naiveté, nor his skepticism, the necessary prelude to faith and complement of it —which, with a believer, is "somehow integrated into the faith which transcends it."

Then, too, Newman and his *Grammar of Assent* were helps to Eliot; and he was already a reader of the mystics, especially of that great Doctor of the *Via Negativa*, St. John of the Cross; but he says, in a final sentence which speaks of an apologist who can reach modern intellectuals, "I can think of no Christian writer, not Newman even, more to be commended than Pascal to those who doubt, but have the mind to conceive, and the sensibility to feel, the disorder, the futility, the meaninglessness, the mystery of life, and suffering and who can only find peace through a satisfaction of the whole being." Elsewhere in the essay, Eliot speaks of "the whole personality" as being involved in the sequence which ends in faith.

It is not by a single argument, like that from Design, which he does not even mention, nor by the evidence from miracles (which impressed Pascal) that the mind is converted. The "modern liberal Catholic" founds his belief in the miracles on the Gospel, not his belief in the Gospel on the miracles, and is much more impressed by the moral authority of conscience and the phenomenon of saintliness and the presence of other 'values' inexplicable by naturalistic philosophies. And so, "by what Newman calls 'powerful and concurrent reasons,' he finds himself committed to the dogma of the Incarnation." The case for the religious interpretation of life cannot be demonstrated. There is a final hiatus between the "powerful and concurrent reasons" and the act of faith, which is an act of the will, of the heart, of the total personality. On Eliot's part, it was certainly an act of will as well as of the mind, a commitment.

At almost the same time that he became an Anglican, he also became a British citizen—a concurrence which might, in a different century and with a different man, have suggested that Church was a subdivision of State (*Cujus regio; eius religio*); but, in his case, it certainly meant no more and no less than that at a given time he decided to put an end to waverings and take a stand, make an election, assume the responsibilities of a participant in civil and spiritual affairs as well as in that third realm already his, the realm of literature.

Thus Eliot, essentially not only a shy man but a solitary, became, by election, the maintainer of institutions; even in literature, he was not only the poet but the active member of a publishing firm and the editor of a review, *The Criterion* (1922–39), with a policy of representing European writers and encouraging young poets as well as providing a quarterly "Commentary" on affairs of Church, State, and Letters.

The immediate effect of his conversion on Eliot as a prose writer was strong, and marked, for something like the next ten years. According to his own grouping, *Selected Essays* (edition of 1950), Section VI, essays written between 1926 and 1935, include the "Pascal," the essays on the Anglican divines, Andrewes and Bramhall, which led off *For Lancelot Andrewes* (1928), "Thoughts after Lambeth," and "Religion and Literature." *Thoughts after Lambeth*, originally published as a brochure after a council of bishops of the worldwide Anglican Church had convened and issued a joint statement on matters of faith and morals, has its technical interest to the ecclesiastical and the social historian, and does much to define Eliot's particular, carefully thought out and by no means extravagant brand of Catholic ('High Church') Anglicanism; but in the company of the other pieces in his 460 page *Selected Essays*, it seems rather grotesquely out of place—both sectarian and provincial.

The same cannot be said of the paper on "Religion and

Literature" written originally for a symposium by Canon V. A. Demant, one of Eliot's later authorities, and called *The Faith That Illuminates* (1935). The first paragraph contains the propositional statements that "Literary criticism should be completed by criticism from a definite ethical and theological standpoint." (Ethics and theology are not, for Eliot as for Arnold, separable parts: all systems or habits of ethics are derivation from a theology and cannot indefinitely survive the abolition of that theology.) And "The greatness" of literature cannot be determined solely by literary standards; though we must remember that whether it is literature or not can be determined' only by "literary standards." (There are two questions, one of the genuineness of literature, a matter for aesthetic judgment, and another, that of rank, which requires the addition of ethical and theological judgments.) At least, this must be the case with "all Christians."

This essay attempts the work of a treatise, raises more questions than it answers, and seems at many points in contradiction to Eliot's statements elsewhere. For example, it seems to divide literature into form and style on the one hand and content and philosophy on the other. And of the two rival views, that art is an imitation which 'catharsizes' and that art is an imitation which incites to imitation, that art is propaganda, Eliot here comes down heavily on the latter side. His strongest point (not original, of course, though he seems to make it as though it were) is that it is popular novels—read passively and for amusement, which may have "the greatest and least suspected influence upon us" (with its corollary, implied not stated, that it is people who read and have read little, the relatively uneducated, who are most affected by the books they chance to read, making, as they do, the least distinction between 'life' and art).

Who is to "complete" literary (i.e., formal) criticism by theological criticism—one and the same man, whether man of letters who is theologically grounded, or theologian who has minored in literature (like the Anglican monk, Fr. Jarrett-Kerr, one of whose books Eliot prefaced)? Eliot nowhere clearly answers this question—if, indeed, he ever so formulated it. In this particular essay he seems to be addressing the general educated Christian reader and inviting him to perform both functions.

On the other hand, *After Strange Gods*, published the year before this essay, seems to give a different answer to the question; for here Eliot, himself an already eminent literary critic, ascends the platform at the University of Virginia "only in the role of a moralist," to demonstrate to those who have never applied "moral or theological principles to literature quite explicitly" that it can be done, by himself applying them to some approximately contemporary writers—Yeats, Joyce, Hardy, and Lawrence. Though it naturally contains some insights and memorable statements, the book (published, as required by the terms of the lectureship) was not reprinted by Eliot, who, though continuing to believe that Christian readers should not read contemporary literature, including his own, without being on their ethical guard, felt, as he confesses in a letter about the book addressed to More, his own particular demonstration to have been inept.

Included with the pieces in Section VI already referred to should be the 1932 essay, an address, called "Modern Education and the Classics"—the first of Eliot's writings on these two topics and the most downright and astringent. Quite in line with the views of P. E. More and of Irving Babbitt (whose first book, *Literature and the American College*, is both an attack on the elective system inaugurated at Harvard by President C. W. Eliot and a strong defense of Greek and Latin), Eliot denounces what passes for liberal education (the view that one subject is as good, for education, as another, and that every one should study what interests him most). But time has moved on, and there are new notes in Eliot's treatment on the subject. There is, for example, an 'anti-democratic' and bitter passage on 'education for leisure' which is written with contemptuous precision. The "majority of people are incapable of enjoying leisure—that is, unemployment *plus* an income and a status of respectability—in any but pretty simple forms—such as balls propelled by hand, by foot, and by engines or tools of various types; in playing cards; or in watching dogs, horses or other men engage in feats of skill or speed." And the final pages of the essay dismiss any arguments for the classics such as might have satisfied nineteenth-century Englishmen or such defenders of humanism as Babbitt. All education, "as only the Catholic and the communist know," is ultimately religious education; and the defense of the classics must rest upon their association with the Catholic "hypothesis" about life, as must, too, any defense of the primacy of the contemplative over the active life. And, finally, "the only hope I can see for the study of Latin and Greek, in their proper place and for the right reasons, lies in the revival and expansion of monastic teaching orders," the first educational duty of which is to preserve education "within the cloister, uncontaminated by the deluge of barbarism outside. . . ."

III

Surveying such essays, one is not surprised to find Eliot writing, for the *Harvard Advocate* of September 1934, in an essay, "The Problems of Education," "At the present time I am not very much interested in the only subject which I am supposedly qualified to write about: that is, one kind of literary criticism" ("pure literary criticism" he calls that kind in a letter of similar purport written to More after the two series of American lectures). "I am not very much interested in literature, except dramatic literature; and I am largely interested in subjects which I do not yet know very much about: theology, politics, economics, and education."

This statement has, of course—for all its seeming candor and nonchalance—much of Eliot's exactness: in "at the present time" and "not very much" and "one kind," as well as in the precision with which his extraliterary interests are specified. No corresponding statement of a later date exists; but what took place thereafter was no abdication of literature or literary criticism. What Mrs. Eliot calls her husband's "sociological writings" (which I take to mean his *Aims of Education* and other educational papers, as well as *The Idea of a Christian So-*

ciety and *Notes towards a Definition of Culture*) went on concurrently, until the end, with both poetry (*The Four Quartets*) and verse plays and literary criticism.

Of the writings on society and education, it is sufficient here to say none has the intransigent tone of "Modern Education and the Classics," an address first delivered, it is to be observed, not before a community of Anglican Benedictines but before the Classical Club of Harvard. The later pieces, and especially the *Notes* on culture, the best of them, are more moderate, if never really conciliatory. The general comment to be made on Eliot's positions is that they should not be taken as representative either of contemporary Anglicanism or contemporary Christian thought, as they appear to be taken by those not much interested in or informed about either.

They are possible positions, urged by an educated and serious man, but one who by temperament was low-spirited, low in 'animal spirits,' ungregarious—by temperament as well as conviction distrustful of the world and the flesh and genuinely fearful of the devil—a world-fleeing man who looked at best with pity on the majority of his fellows and who loved them 'in God', not by any natural instinct. By temperament he was a contemplative, an endurer, not an activist; and his religion brought him peace but not joy. (As he rightly said his poetry could not express ideals but experience; and the *Four Quartets* includes no *Paradiso*. But abstractly, in his prose, he could transcend his temperament.)

The *Notes* on culture is probably the most considered and reasonable defense of Conservatism now available. It proposes a state in which an *elite* of intellect and talent, necessarily uncontinuous, is counterbalanced by a hereditary aristocracy, representing both continuity and character, such social responsibility as is approximately transmissible. It sensibly holds that the highest kind of education cannot be given to all, that the degree as well as kind of education will have to be determined by class, both social and intellectual: equality is not justice. And it maintains that a community is bound together by its culture (which is the incarnation in customs and sensibility of its real as distinct from its avowed religion): popular culture (culture in the anthropological sense) is continuous with and finds intellectual articulation in the culture of the upper classes. And, finally, the *Notes* best exposits the view, long implicit in Eliot's writings, that the modern National State represents but one stage in the ordered series which extends from the village to the region (Wales, Scotland, Yorkshire) to Europe (which includes England). Large grandiose 'universals' (in which principles unite) and governments which are 'representative' must be balanced against local and regional governments with direct participation and corresponding regional cultures. The book includes no practical suggestions as to how to bring about such a State. It is the presentation of an Idea of Society still partially exemplified by England (even to an Established Church and a monarchy, both of which—when still extant—Eliot thought desirable); it is a plea to save and preserve what remains of an everywhere threatened order, and an attempt intellectually to define the principles which, however imperfectly, such an order exemplifies.

This book, which has had intellectual commendation even from those in little sympathy with its ideas, is probably the best of Eliot's writings on subjects outside the range of his professional competences. Among its other virtues, it stands as evidence of Eliot's responsible citizenship, his attempt at overtly supporting the systems of civilization which had not only made his own career possible but had made possible the functioning of the arts and specifically the art of poetry.

Eliot had never supposed art not to "serve ends beyond itself" but only that art "is not required to be aware of these ends, and indeed performs its function . . . much better by indifference to them"—and that, as art is not a substitute for anything else—whether sex, society, or religion—so no one of these is a substitute for it. Basic to Eliot's constitutional way of thinking is the assumption that there is a certain number of basic activities and interests and values—how many he never

Connections

presumes to number or name. An ideal society, a Platonic re-
public or an ideal or idealized, medieval world, includes them
all, in proportion and hierarchy.

I V

In 1957 Eliot published *On Poetry and Poets*, a collection of
literary-critical essays written subsequently to those in *Selected Essays*, originally published in 1932. Like its predecessor, this book is the author's own selection; and another critic
may regret both inclusions and omissions—among the former,
the address on "Goethe as the Sage," in which Eliot, repelled
by the great German poet, yet aware there must be reasons
for admiring him, is largely, and embarrassingly, reduced to an
autobiographical account of his own traffic with this world-
figure—and among the omissions the distinguished essay,
"From Poe to Valéry," separately published as far back as 1948
(and later included in the posthumous and rather too miscellaneous volume *To Criticize the Critic*, 1965). One familiar with
checklists of Eliot's essays, book reviews, and many prefaces
written for books of others will miss the 1946 essay on Pound,
that on *Ulysses*, that on Marianne Moore, and so on. It was
Eliot's principle to collect none of these pieces on his contemporaries—perhaps out of caution, perhaps because, as he
said, he believed a contemporary had not perspective enough
to assign permanent rank, but could attest only to literary
'genuineness'—though this seems really no adequate reason why
Eliot (who as a matter of fact included an essay on Yeats in
On Poetry and Poets) should doubt the value of putting on
permanent record his own provisional estimates, his warranted
'appreciations,' of his contemporaries.

But with this puzzlement over inclusions and exclusions
one is familiar. The impressive and reassuring thing about *On
Poetry* is its evidence that, though his sense of social responsibility—what might be called his assumption of the full Arnoldian role—had increased, Eliot showed himself continuingly
capable of literary judgment and discernment.

The essays in the earlier volume were chiefly written to

170

be read by the private eye; those in *On Poetry* (like the chapters of *The Use of Poetry*) to be listened to by public audiences. The essays were the products of a poet writing primarily for himself; the lectures addressed an audience assembled to hear a topic discussed, and discussed with a certain authority, by a distinguished and famous man. For in the last fifteen or twenty years of his life, Eliot was an eminence, and that not merely among poets and literary men—among whom he was an 'elder statesman.' He now felt free to be more 'personal' as well as retrospective; now overtly presented as his own experience what, at any earlier time (as in the Pascal essay), he would have left to be surmised as such. To say 'I' instead of 'one' may be either modest or proud: it is often some combination of both.

Mr. Ransom has called Eliot a "historical critic" and has asserted that "The University should have produced scores of Eliots [men who turn their scholarship to "pointed critical uses"] so far as his kind of intelligence is concerned, though one might wish to make reservations about its quickness, or its depth, which would probably be superior in any age," and points to Dr. Johnson as his congener.

In the essay on "Johnson as a Critic and Poet," Eliot has provided a really superior piece of literary-historical criticism, so exemplary in method that one wishes he had written more such studies, and, specifically, corresponding studies of the two poet-critics he names as of equal rank with Johnson—Dryden and Coleridge. The method consists of applying to a group of 'period' poems the critical theory and standards of the great critic of the period. Eliot set himself to read the poets who were, at Johnson's instigation, added to the poets the booksellers had proposed including in their set of the British poets. He read Sir Richard Blackmore's *Creation: A Philosophic Poem;* he read carefully, too, those writers of blank verse—notably, Akenside—whom Johnson exempted from his general indictment of blank verse. The attempt is to understand Johnson's praise, together with its reserves, and to apply both to a poem, or a passage from a poem, by the poet at hand. Such an exercise, like studies in 'sources and influences' which transcend the mechanical, is work not for apprentices but for the most sensitive and mature scholar-critic.

In praising Akenside's *Pleasures of the Imagination*, Johnson said: "with the philosophical or religious tenets of the author I have nothing to do; my business is with the poetry." And, as a matter of fact, his hostile comments on Milton's doctrine and character, as well as those on other poets, are to be found in the *Lives*, always discretely separated from the critical analysis and judgment of the poet's works. It was a part of the nostalgic envy with which Eliot viewed Johnson that he "was in a position, as no critic of equal stature has been since, to write purely literary criticism, just because he was able to assume that there was [in his time] a general attitude towards life, and a common opinion as to the place of poetry in it."

Three more essays in *On Poetry* require special attention. They are distinctly 'later' essays; lack the brilliance and audacity of the early masterpieces, "Tradition and the Individual Talent," "The Metaphysical Poets," and "Andrew Marvell." They develop and bring to fulfillment another side of Eliot, present from the start in that first book of essays, *The Sacred Wood: Essays on Poetry and Criticism*, with its critical essays on poets and its critical essays on critics. Eliot was a criticizer of the critics from the beginning; and he learned the art of criticism from the critics as he learned the art of poetry from the poets. The three 'later essays' are "What Is Minor Poetry?" and "What Is a Classic?"—both of 1944, and "The Frontiers of Criticism" (1956). I. A. Richards might well have illustrated by these essays the fine remark he made in a memorial characterization of Eliot: "Few minds have more enjoyed the process of pondering a discrimination: pondering it rather than formulating it or maintaining it. . . ." These essays are such ponderings.

The 1944 essays form a kind of pair, and complement each other, both having to do with both order and hierarchy. They complement, but there is no neat matching or correspondence; for 'major,' and not 'classic,' is the strict antonym of 'minor.' There hovers the distinction between genuine literature, whatever its rank, and 'great' literature, a distinction which is never quite precipitated: we may infer that all classics must be great literature though not all great books are classics.

"What Is Minor Poetry" opens with the warning, "I do not propose to offer, either at the beginning or the end, a definition of minor poetry": the stress is on the article, for many tentative and, for specific purposes useful, definitions are offered. And "What Is a Classic?" opens similarly with the statement, "I do not aim to supersede, or to outlaw, any use of the word 'classic' which precedent has made permissible. The word has, and will continue to have, several meanings in several contexts: I am concerned with one meaning in one context." All key words in criticism must be understood contextually. A critic does his part by making the context as clear as he can: the rest of the semantic transaction must be managed by the reader. In Eliot's case, the context is the specific essay and its occasion: that on the Classic, being addressed to the Virgil Society, may be expected, as Eliot says, to define 'classic' in such a way as to include, and illuminate, the case of Virgil.

The occasional context of defining 'minor' (and 'major') has to be inferred; but the centrality of the discussion of George Herbert's case—the pondering whether or not he is adequately represented by four or five anthology pieces, or is, despite his having written no single long poem, a major poet, a question of latter-day concern to Eliot—seems to offer the contextual key. To the traditional view that major poets are those who, like Virgil and Dante, have written major poems, long poems (epics or the equivalent), Eliot, in transit, agrees as true of "the very greatest poets"; but for majorness it is only necessary that the poet (e.g., Herbert) has written a structured sequence of short poems, which, like *The Temple*, gives the "feeling of a unifying personality" and gains immeasurably if known as a "whole work" and not as so many selected pieces.

"What Is a Classic?" has been cited by Dr. Leavis as giving one a sense of "a strenuous *academic* quality; the sense of an intensity of intellectual energy . . . incommensurate with any upshot of defined, organized, and profitable thought"; and I quote Dr. Leavis because my own first reaction to the essay was not dissimilar. Many subtle distinctions are made in the essay; and there is certainly a sense that Eliot is impelled to such distinctions by some deep, powerful feeling; but what is he so 'intense' about, and of what use, either to a practicing poet or a practicing teacher of literature, is what he has to say? Of no immediate practical or technical use to either, it must be replied; but of long-range usefulness to both.

Eliot has not, as his audience might have expected, attempted to defend or exalt the teaching and study of Latin and Greek. Nor is he attempting to defend a timeless classicism against either a period Romanticism or a perennial 'romantic spirit.' Eliot had been reared by Irving Babbitt as an anti-Romanticist, and, with the further aid of ideas from Maurras and Hulme and others, he had, in his famous Preface, described his point of view as "classicist in literature"; but, he added immediately in the Preface, "I am quite aware that the . . . term is completely vague, and easily lends itself to clap-trap." In this essay of 1944, he dismisses 'classic' and 'romantic' as "a pair of terms" belonging to "literary politics"—the term "classical" meaning, according to which party uses it, "either the perfection of form, or the absolute zero of frigidity."

It is much to be doubted that, even when Eliot called himself a "classicist in literature," he meant by classicism anything more specific than 'critical perspective.' He certainly never called his own poetry 'classical' in any such sense as that in which Paul Elmer More (or Yvor Winters) found him 'romantic' or 'wonderful' or 'symbolist'; nor did he ever disavow or ignore his Romantic-Imagist-Symbolist poetic lineage (to which were collaterally added Metaphysical and Neoclassical elements). To be a 'classical' poet in an unclassical age (i.e., an age which has no "common style" because it has no coherent culture) is necessarily different from being a classical poet in a classical age.

Of the dictionary senses of 'classic,' Eliot certainly intends, in his essay, the primary—of the first class, that excellence in whatever sphere which gives the standard from which all other classes derive their degree of subordination. But, assuming that, he offers as the one word which suggests the maximum meaning of the term for him, the word *maturity;* and this is so ultimate a concept that it cannot be defined except circularly: we have to assume that 'mature' hearers already know what maturity means. Its concrete primary meaning is organic, agricultural, biological, psychological; then, by natural extension, it is applied to civilization, to language, to literature—perhaps to philosophy as 'view of life' (cf. Eliot's remarks on maturity in 'view of life' when he discusses, and dismisses, Shelley in *The Use of Poetry and the Use of Criticism*). Eliot recognizes that "to make the meaning of maturity really apprehensible—indeed, even to make it acceptable—to the immature, is perhaps impossible."

These are understatements. In the world Eliot lived in, and we live in, even should there be any general agreement on what persons and cultures, and what works of art, are 'mature,' there are many barbarians, and some art connoisseurs, who clearly and expressly prefer primitivism and the archaic or the decadent, the underripe or the overripe. What argument against, or with, such? What argument, indeed, can there be about 'first principles'? And it is with first principles that Eliot is concerned in this essay—the first principles of theory, or of conviction, which lie behind or beneath all profitable practical criticism.

This essay is Eliot's most seriously felt and coherently thought out attempt at latter-day statement of his total position—the widest in scope and the least sectarian. It covers, and brings together, the aesthetic and the ethical, manners and language, tradition and the individual poetic talent as he had not succeeded in doing since that first famous and 'classic' essay with which he began his career.

"The Frontiers of Criticism" was first delivered at the University of Minnesota in 1956, before the largest audience Eliot ever addressed: reputedly, twenty thousand people, mostly students, who had gathered together to hear the most famous New Critic or at least ancestor of the New Critics. This is a lecture less grave and weighty than "What Is a Classic?"—indeed, a kind of high-class journalism, easy and sometimes jocular or chatty in tone, with considerable literary autobiography and some analyzed examples of different types of scholarly criticism and literary scholarship (e.g., Lowes's *Road to Xanadu* and Sir Herbert Read's and "a Mr. Bateson's" use of biography in interpreting the poetry of Wordsworth).

The lecture, published, did not, at least upon first reading, please Eliot's fellow critics. It appeared a lowering of the seriousness with which their common pursuit had been followed in *The Sacred Wood;* Eliot, who had done so much to inaugurate and dignify literary criticism, appeared now trying to demote it. The 'close reading' of poems, which his own poetry required, and which his own criticism of poetry had exemplified, was now called, at least as practiced by the younger academics, "the lemon-squeezer school of criticism." Further, he appeared to dismiss his theoretical essays like "Tradition and the Individual Talent" by the reference to "a few notorious phrases which have had a truly embarrassing success in the world," and he limited the best of his "literary criticism" to essays on poets and poetic dramatists who had influenced him, the by-products of his "private poetry-workshop." The old dogmatism and audacity are absent from this lecture as well as the close writing of "The Metaphysical Poets." Eliot has become so tolerant, even appreciative, of the varieties of literary criticism, so willing to extend the "frontiers" (to use his politico-military metaphor) that we may forget (what comes out clearly in the pendant "To Criticize the Critic") that for him the center of the country, the farthest from frontier peril, remains the criticism of poetry written by a poet.

Subsequent readings will discern a good deal of common sense, and practical wisdom, and tactical perspective in the essay, the 'text' of which, plainly and accurately pronounced in the first sentence, is "that there are limits, exceeding which in one direction literary criticism ceases to be literary and exceeding which in another it ceases to be criticism." Eliot acknowledges the changes which have taken place since, in *The Sacred Wood*, he inveighed against Impressionistic criticism (with its overemphasis on appreciation, the enjoyment of literature). Now, in 1956, it seems to him that criticism overemphasizes understanding, an understanding which, in turn, is slipping into "mere explanation": either 'explication' or the reductive process which attributes the poetry to biographical or sociological 'causes': criticism is turning into a form of academic scholarship and even pretending to be a "science, which it never can be." And common to the old Impressionism and the New Objectivism is the neglect of *evaluation*. (Eliot never uses the word; but what else are we to call understanding and enjoying a poem "to the right degree and in the right way, relative to the other poems"?)

Perhaps the real surprise of the lecture lies in its assertion —which carries us beyond the workshop criticism of 'the poet as critic'—that a literary critic need not be "purely" literary. "A critic who was interested in nothing but 'literature' would have very little to say to us, for his literature would be pure abstraction." Like the poet himself, he must have other interests; "for the literary critic is not merely a technical expert . . . : the critic must be the whole man, a man with convictions and principles, and knowledge and experience of life"—a definition with which no humanist can disagree. Such a man would indeed be what Eliot desiderated in the opening essay of *The Sacred Wood*, the "perfect critic"—though it is likely that Aristotle as well as Remy de Gourmont had been displaced by 1956 from the exemplary positions they held in that earlier essay.

v

"To Criticize the Critic," delivered at the University of Leeds in 1961, reviews Eliot's own literary criticism, both practical and theoretical, his essays on particular poets and poet-dramatists and those on theory of poetry and theory of criticism. In a sense it is an extension of the Minnesota lecture on the

"Frontiers of Criticism," even more autobiographical than it
but less bent on being 'popular,' in tone more serious.

This self-criticism is a document of considerable interest
and value, to which I know no very close equivalent—not, certainly, Henry James's prefaces to the New York edition; for
the equivalent of that would have been, what Eliot seems
never to have planned, a history of the composition of his own
poems, accompanied by discussion of the problems of composition they presented, and concluded by his estimate, at the
end of his life, of their relative worth. Something of this sort
he does in section two, of "Poetry and Drama," with his comments on his "intentions, failures, and partial successes" in his
plays. But *Prufrock, Gerontion, The Waste Land,* and *Four
Quartets,* the center of his poetic achievement, his Unpublic
Poems, probably remained too intimately tied to his personal
life for him to treat them in the only way he would have felt
possible—in terms of their technical devices.

Eliot clearly asserts that he does not think of himself as
the "philosophical critic" like Richards, or "the Critic as Moralist" like Dr. Leavis, or the "Professional Critic" like his
friend P. E. More, but as the poet-critic whose criticism is a
"by-product of his creative activity." In his opinion, indeed,
his own criticism has not had, and could not have had, "any
influence whatever" apart from the poems; and he is certain
that he has written best about the writers who have influenced
his own poetry—including not only poets but prose writers
like Lancelot Andrewes and F. H. Bradley.

He is, at this point, insistent on the purely literary residue
of his close reading and exposition of Bradley—"whose personality as manifested in his works—affected me profoundly";
and, as against any hypothetical expositors who may interpret
Eliot's criticism in the light of his metaphysical and epistemological training, he asserts, "I spent three years, when young,
in the study of philosophy. What remains to me of these studies? The style of three philosophers: Bradley's English, Spinoza's Latin and Plato's Greek."

As for his theorizing, he was never doing more than generalizing his own sensibility, his own tastes; and the celebrated phrases like "dissociation of sensibility" and "objective correlative" were but "conceptual symbols for emotional preferences."

On the topic of Continuity and Coherence in his critical thought and writing, he has his own opinion to give. He objects to having forty years of 'occasional' writing reduced to simultaneous existence. One very intelligent and sympathetic expositor has, he says, written "as if I had, at the onset of my career as a literary critic, sketched out the design for a massive critical structure, and spent the rest of my life filling in the details," while he intended his very habit of printing the original dates of his essays to prevent such a misconception. Yet this objection to neglecting the occasional contexts of his essays is more than balanced by his statements on the side of continuity and coherence. Rereading his own earlier essays as "required reading" for the lecture he was to give, he found he could still "identify" himself as their author, even in the errors or tone, "the braggadocio of the mild-mannered man safely entrenched behind his typewriter." He found, as any critic will, in rereading his own old work, views he now maintains "with less firmness of conviction," or only with reservations, statements the meaning of which he no longer understands, and some matters in which he has simply lost interest, even in whether he still holds the same belief or not—in other words, shifts of interest and of emphasis; but no radical break or disastrous incoherence.

But—it today goes almost without being said—Eliot's 'intentions,' Eliot's interpretation of his own work, and his estimate of the relative value of its parts have no binding power on others who "criticize the critic"; they are testimony valuable to have but possess no absolute authority. It is to be remarked, for example, that Eliot's attitude toward his early philosophic studies, though partly ambiguous (he did, after all permit the eventual printing of his Harvard doctoral dissertation, *Knowledge and Experience in the Philosophy of F. H.*

Bradley), is largely skeptical and hostile; he is largely dubious of their value to him, and seems even generally dubious of systems of abstract thought; he repeatedly also, and, it would seem, not entirely in Arnoldianly ironic modesty, declares himself incapable of systematic abstract thinking; and this repudiation of metaphysics as something verbalistic and academic appears at least as strongly at the beginning of his career as a writer (example, in *The Perfect Critic*) as at the end—though presumably fear of having to become a professor of philosophy rather than doubt of his ability to be one made him prefer to be a banking clerk. Yet plausible cases have already been made for the influence on Eliot, as poet and critic, not only by —what he admits—the style and literary 'personality' of Bradley but by Bradley's philosophy.

Even before Eliot's death, there began to exist a large amount of interpretative commentary on his criticism—as well as his poetry; and there has been very considerable disagreement among able fellow critics, including Ransom, Tate, Winters, and Leavis. The issues disputed are, principally, the degree to which Eliot's religious conversion altered his critical position: whether, from being a purely aesthetic critic he became a moral one, or a combination of both; and whether, if there was a change, it was a break or a shift of emphasis; then, whether Eliot's criticism is full of self-contradictions, or, instead, reasonably coherent, or even—in essence, if not in form of presentation—methodical and coherent enough to be called systematic; and, finally, perhaps, whether the prime value of his criticism lies in its theory, or theoretical implications, or whether it lies rather in his corruscation of 'insights.'

These topics and discussions have been ably summarized in "The Commentators' Vistas," the Introduction to *T. S. Eliot: The Dialectical Structure of His Theory of Poetry*, Fei-Pai Lu's Chicago doctoral dissertation, published in 1966. Mr. Lu's book, which professedly "aims to exhibit rather than to evaluate Eliot's critical theory," by exhibiting it, raises its total and final value; and—what is not the same thing—it as well exhibits Eliot's critical thought as having, from its earliest writing on, a degree of coherence which, without the demonstration, would have seemed incredible. By the dialectical method (in which, as a student of Plato and Bradley, Eliot certainly had been trained) the seeming oppositions of art and morality, the personal and the impersonal, feeling and thought, are shown to be reconciled and transcended. Lu's book has the further value of wide quotations from Eliot's often brilliant early pieces, as yet uncollected.

It may, of course, be said that Lu makes Eliot into a systematic.thinker by the strategy of quoting passages from four decades of critical writing as though their dates and contexts had no bearing upon their interpretation; and Mr. David Huisman, who has studied Eliot's criticism chronologically and, as one might say, biographically, justly makes this charge—without however denying, indeed ably and usefully demonstrating, that Eliot's post-1928 attitudes, with their adjustment of the aesthetic and the ethical, were adumbrated almost from the start, notably in the reviews of philosophical and theological books which he published in 1916 and 1917.

The distinguished historian of modern criticism, Dr. Wellek, who values systematic thought and does not readily concede it to critics, however acute or sensitive some of their occasional perceptions may be (see, for example, his treatment of De Quincey), wrote in 1956 of Eliot: he "has been constantly working at a general theory, and from the very beginning has had a theory at the back of his mind"; and, again, "his theory of poetry . . . is much more coherent and systematic than most commentators have allowed." On the other hand, Allen Tate, in 1949, gave as a reason for thinking Eliot "still" perhaps "our best critic because his constant frames of reference [his theories] are loose and large, the frame of the particular essay being improvised, tentative, and variable. . . ."

In my own 1940 essay on Eliot, now constituting the first section of the present one, I spoke of "schematic outlines" as doing him "a special injustice" and found his "characteristic virtue" not primarily in "perspective"—by which I meant large, general ideas, theory. The studies of Huisman and Lu have somewhat altered my position. After reading these impressive studies, it is impossible to deny that, despite a flexible terminology and shifts in emphasis, there is, throughout Eliot's work, a substantial unity and coherence of thought; if not a system of conscious thought, then a coherence of conscience and 'sensibility,' a persistent *Strebung* toward a structural articulation of a serious man's emotions, feelings, perceptions, and purposes.

This must not be read as a 'strategy' or a 'program,' or rendered too conscious. If Eliot had ambitions to system-building, he would certainly have taken pains to read over his own earlier work and retrospectively explain or justify at least seeming contradictions and inconsistencies: his repeated statements, till the last essay, that he has not read over his earlier work, seem arrogant on the part of a publishing and eminent critic. But his intention was other, I think: he sought for no merely verbal or even overtly logical consistency but one which should depend on the constant maintenance of spiritual integrity. And so, though he treats each of his prose pieces as 'occasional,' his mind is possessed by the occupation with a steady series of central topics. And each time he takes one of these up, he starts afresh to think it out, hoping to advance his development of thought on this topic, and trusting that his mind has such a reasonable degree of continuity and coherence that there will be no really shocking break but some advance, at least some new distinctions and refinements.

Eliot has been called an 'empirical critic,' and so he is. He knew the kind of aesthetician who constructs his categories out of a minimal experience of little-enjoyed artifacts, and had a just horror of such. But an empirical critic is not required to dispense with literary theory—only to make sure that his theories do not go beyond his own literary experience, including (for he is not a solipsist) his experience of the experience of others.

In Eliot's criticism there is, at least *in potentia*, a theoretical generalization of his experience as so defined, and that is all to the good. But—and there his past (and perhaps more impressionist)—readers have been accurate: the dominant, the crowning achievement lies in the vitality, vivacity, and copiousness of his perceptions and insights—the constant and invigorating sense of a first-rate mind intent upon the process of thinking.

1966 [1969]

Notes

Chiefly Bibliographical

The Very Reverend Dr. John Donne

This essay, first published in the *Kenyon Review* in 1954, and an exegesis, "Donne's 'Extasie'" (*Studies in Philology*, July 1958), are the two visible remains of a long-continued study of Donne's poetry and prose which was to have taken final form in a monograph something on the order of my *Crashaw*.

Of books, articles, and essays read in preparation for the teaching of Donne, which I did during the ten years before this essay was written (teaching which included a course given in 1948 during the ever-memorable first year of the Kenyon School of English), or specifically in preparation for the proposed book, I should like to cite, as especially relevant to this essay on Donne as a churchman and preacher, my debts to Caroline Richardson's *English Preachers and Preaching* . . . (1928); to Evelyn Simpson's *Study of the Prose Works of John Donne* (2d ed., 1948), especially her "Sketch of Donne's Life," a sober and cautious statement; to Mr. Fraser Mitchell's *English Pulpit Oratory from Andrewes to Tillotson* . . . (1932); to Helen C. White's "The Conversions of John Donne" (*The Metaphysical Poets: A Study in Religious Experience*, 1936); to Don Cameron Allen's "Dean Donne Sets His Text" (*ELH*, 1943); and to G. R. Potter's edition of *A Sermon Preached at Lincoln's Inn* . . . (1946), forerunner of the Potter-Simpson edition of *The Sermons* which began to appear in 1953.

I cite the pioneer biography by Dr. Augustus Jessop (*Donne:* 'Great Leaders of Religion' series, 1897) and Itrat-Husain's *Dogmatic and Mystical Theology of Donne* (1938) as giving, in my judgment, quite mistaken conceptions of Donne's theology and churchmanship: the latter, particularly, is to be 'read with caution.'

Logan Pearsall Smith's essay, from which I quote, was first published as an introduction to *Selected Passages* from Donne's Sermons (1920), and is reprinted, together with a similar essay on the sermons and other religious prose of Jeremy Taylor, in Smith's *Reperusals and Re-Collections* (1937).

Edward Le Comte's *Grace to a Witty Sinner* . . . (1965), a really valuable biography of Donne, though unfortunately titled and undocumented, contains a good chapter on "A Preacher in Earnest." William R. Mueller's *John Donne: Preacher* (1962) is competent but rather pedestrian. Joan Webber's brilliant and illuminating *Contrary Music: The Prose Style of John Donne* (1963) opens with the remark, "I think it is fair to say that in the pulpit Donne achieved his fullest artistic expression. . . ."

My quotations from Donne's sermons originally followed the only then available modern text of Dean Henry Alford's *Works of Donne* (1839). They have now been corrected to follow that of the Potter-Simpson edition of the sermons (1953–62) and the John Sparrow edition of *Devotions* (1923), though I have modernized my excerpts.

The Styles of Sir Thomas Browne

"This essay was prompted by the sense that Browne, much written on (and most frequently and ably in the last three decades), still lacked integral treatment: he had been studied as a figure in the history of ideas (whether religious or scientific or both), and he had been considered by narrowly stylistic methods—methods dealing with his rhythm or his diction in disjunction from the meaning in which—unless mere ornament—

they must participate. Viewing *style* as *expressive*, as an aspect of *meaning*, I have tried to bring the "mind" and the "music" of Browne into some kind of correlation.

"My conscious debts are substantial: on stylistics, to E. A. Tenney and Craig La Drière, to Spitzer, Wellek, and Wimsatt; on the style of Browne, to the work of Morris Croll, J. Loiseau's "Sir Thomas Browne, Ecrivain Métaphysique," W. Murison's edition of *Hydriotaphia* (1922), E. L. Parker's "The Cursus in Sir Thomas Browne," and to Norton Temple's "Rhythm in the Prose of Sir Thomas Browne" (I draw my examples of Browne's cadences from Croll, Parker, and Tempest); on Browne as "thinker," to W. P. Dunn's *Browne: A Study in Religious Philosophy* (1926; revised ed., 1950), E. S. Merton's *Science and Imagination in Browne* (1949), Joseph Needham's *The Great Amphibium* (1931), Basil Willey's *Seventeenth Century Background* (1934), and D. K. Ziegler, *In Distinguished and Divided Worlds* (1943)."

The preceding paragraphs were appended to this essay when it appeared (1951) in the *Kenyon Review*. I should like to add that my reference to Wimsatt was particularly to the early essay, "Style as Meaning," which serves as Introduction to his *Prose Style of Samuel Johnson* (1941); that George Saintsbury's discussion of *Urn Burial* is to be found in his *History of English Prose Rhythms* (1912); that Morris Croll's "Baroque Style in Prose" can now be read in the collected essays of this American master of stylistics, *Style, Rhetoric, and Rhythm* . . . , edited, with rich prefaces and notes, by J. Max Patrick, and others (1966).

Two excellent books on Browne, both of which take comprehensive account of preceding scholarship, and 'transcend by including,' are recent: Frank Huntley's *Sir Thomas Browne* (1962) and Leonard Nathanson's *The Strategy of Truth: A Study of Sir Thomas Browne* (1967). The latter attempts, with considerable success, to consider Browne's work under the three-fold illumination of "literary history, the history of ideas, and modern critical theory."

The standard edition of *The Works of Sir Thomas Browne*

is Geoffrey Keynes' (1931). Vol. VI of the *Works* collects Browne's letters; and the one I quote, written in 1679, runs on pp. 160–62.

Frank L. Huntley's excellent 'Everyman's Library' edition of the *Religio Medici And Other Writings* (1951) is the most useful for the general reader.

Dr. Cotton Mather's Magnalia

In a chapter of *The New England Conscience*, I made use of Mather's *Diary*, and my intent was to portray the neurotic aspects of this complex man, including his pseudo-mysticism. In this essay, written at the same time and judged to be compatible with the other, I turn my eyes toward Mather's strength, toward his Big Book, which was to present, to the Reformed Churches of England and Europe and to his own decadent contemporaries, the inspiring history of New England's Founding Fathers—to write their Exodus, their Judges, and their Leviticus, together with some Prophecies and some hint of Revelation. The Book is a mixture of epic, history, and homily; and, marred though it is, it remains a book of considerable imaginative power, a New England mythology.

The 'stratagem' of this essay, its coming at Mather by passage through the nineteenth-century New England authors, reproduces my own literary experience, which began by discovering the importance to Hawthorne of the Mathers' writings. A full study (not merely a compilation) of Cotton Mather's use by nineteenth and twentieth-century imaginative writers, philosophers, and historians would be worth the making.

The phrase quoted from Mrs Stowe comes from her *Oldtown Folks* (1869, 229, toward the end of Chapter XIX). Mrs. Stowe (especially in this novel, which abounds in meditative passages of historic and psychological insight) is the indispensable interpreter of the New England conscience and consciousness as shaped by their regional past; an excellent commentary is C. H. Foster's *Rungless Ladder: H. B. Stowe and New England Puritanism* (1954).

Notes

Mather's *Magnalia* I have read in Reverend Dr. Thomas Robbins' edition published at Hartford in 1852, photostatically reproduced in 1967 by Russell and Russell. The *Magnalia* needs fuller annotation than it has yet been given; and it is good to learn that Professor Kenneth Murdock is preparing such an edition. Murdock remains, though a witness for the defense, our best scholarly authority for both Cotton Mather and his father, Increase. I have made use of his excellent introduction to *Selections from Cotton Mather* (1926) and his *Literature and Theory in Colonial New England* (1949). For Mather biography, Barrett Wendell's book subtitled *The Puritan Priest* (1891; reissued, 1963) has not been quite superseded.

On Mather's style, I should like to make reference to Zdenek Vancura's pioneer study, "Baroque Prose in Colonial America," *Studies in English by Members of the English Seminar of Charles University*, IV (1933), 39–58, and an unpublished Michigan doctoral dissertation by William Manierre, II, "Cotton Mather and the Plain Style." And I should like to acknowledge my debt, in thinking out the "Concept of Baroque," to my friend, René Wellek, whose brilliant study of that name may be read in his *Concepts of Criticism* (1963), 54–114.

The "recent judge" of Mather quoted at the end of Section IV is Peter Gay, whose masterly *A Loss of Mastery: Puritan Historians in Colonial America* (1966) concluded by an exemplary "Bibliographical Essay," I have read with profit and delight. Gay's general intellectual position is antithetic to my own; he remarks (p. 121) upon the superiority of "history based on critical thinking" to "history based on myth" ("Puritan history was at heart mythic"); while I (literary man and lay theologian) praise Mather for his accomplishment of a mythic history or a historical mythology. Nonetheless, Gay's chapter on Mather, "A Pathetic Plutarch," though technically a prosecutor's case, is one of the most comprehensive, acute, and even just judgments of Mather that have been made.

To conclude this Note, I offer a few 'connections': William Carlos Williams' *In the American Grain* (1925), a 'mythic' history (designed to counteract the New England view of the matter by playing up the healthy contributions to our national history of the Spanish explorers, the French explorers and missionaries, and the Virginians), includes Cotton Mather, as being the *fons et origo* of the American malady, Puritanism. At Paris, still composing his 'Counterstatement,' Williams was introduced to the well-known French writer Valéry Larbaud and was astonished to discover that the latter had really read the *Magnalia* and with literary admiration: "I began," Williams writes, "to be impatient of my friend's cultured tolerance, the beauties he saw" (*op. cit.*, 107–16).

Robert F. Sayre, in his *The Examined Self: Franklin, Henry Adams, and Henry James* (1964), a sensitively brilliant analysis of three American autobiographies, cites (p. 200) the *Magnalia* as philosophic autobiography, coupling it with *The Education of Henry Adams* and Eliot's *Four Quartets* for its "inclusiveness." This insight deserves to be read in its context.

The Scarlet Letter

This essay has a history which I wish to give. Neither an American literature man, nor a Hawthorne specialist, I was early concerned with the history and literature of my own region, New England, and especially drawn to Hawthorne. When, in 1933, Harry Hayden Clark, editor of the projected 'American Writers Series,' invited me to prepare the Hawthorne volume (selections from the Tales, with Notes and Introduction), I responded eagerly and had my edition ready for publication the following year. And when Rinehart projected its series of paperbacks for college use, I wrote the introduction for their first issue, *The Scarlet Letter* (1947).

My but half-conscious intent in writing the present essay was to discuss Hawthorne's masterpiece as a novel rather than a 'romance' and to ignore the 'symbolism.' The symbolism and the chiaroscuro of multiple interpretations in which Hawthorne delighted are certainly more appropriate—and less fanciful and mannered—in *The Scarlet Letter* than elsewhere in his work, yet even here I could at least half wish them away; and I saw, or seemed to see, that the short, intense novel could well stand simply as a narrative concerned with the "deeper psychology" which James attributes to Hawthorne.

It was an engaging project to sit down to write on a minor masterpiece almost entirely on the basis of rereading, attentively and meditatively, the book itself. A scholar-critic, in his professional modesty, does not presume, like Lawrence, in his *Studies in Classic American Literature*, a preparation so pure, but, before and after reading on his own, corrects and multiplies his vision by the use of biographies and commentaries, the books about books and authors. My case this time was too special to generalize upon, for I had done the scholar's part of my 'homework' long enough ago so that it had receded to being what might be postulated as the right distance for 'background' to take; but it was an enjoyable and enviable experience.

Books about Hawthorne's books proceed apace; and, as Hawthorne is a literary man's novelist, critical insights continue to accumulate. The likely danger is that what was written on his work before the New Criticism and the New Scholarship shall be assumed to be superseded. But literary criticism (like theology and philosophy) is not a 'science' or even, primarily, a technology. It is a collaboration between types of readers and generations of readers; the total meaning of the literary work of art emerges from this collaboration; it accrues.

Accordingly, the older studies of Hawthorne should not be neglected—especially, I think, those written by other writers: I think immediately of Henry James's *Hawthorne* in the 'English Men of Letters' series (1879) and of the very fine early essay on Hawthorne and James by T. S. Eliot (first published as "Henry James: The Hawthorne Aspect" in 1918 and reprinted in Edmund Wilson's valuable anthology *The Shock of Recognition*). Of older essays on Hawthorne I would also especially mention Leslie Stephen's (in *Hours in a Library*, First series, 1874), Paul Elmer More's two (reprinted in Daniel Aaron's *More's Shelburne Essays on American Literature*,

1963), and W. C. Brownell's critically severe chapter in *American Prose Masters* (1909), a neglected but distinguished book. A convenient repertory of selected earlier criticism will be found in Bernard Cohen's *The Recognition of Nathaniel Hawthorne . . .* (1969).

Emily Dickinson

This essay first appeared in the *Sewanee Review* (1957) and was occasioned by the publication, in 1955, of Thomas Johnson's Harvard Variorum edition of Emily Dickinson's Poems; and my opening pages reviewed this epoch-making edition, making some passing comments on previous editions and some suggestions for a 'reader's text' of the poems. As, in its original form, it has several times been reprinted—for example, in R. B. Sewall's *Emily Dickinson: A Collection of Critical Essays*, published (1963) in the series, 'Twentieth Century Views,' I have now recast the essay, omitting the pages of review.

My conscious indebtedness is to George Whicher's *This Was a Poet* (1938) and Millicent Todd Bingham's books, especially *Emily Dickinson's Home* (1955) among biographical studies, and to the critical essays of Allen Tate and Richard Blackmur (the latter, a good astringent to 'appreciation' of E. D. too lush or undiscriminating). My essay owes much to conversations with my late brilliant brother-in-law, the Boston poet, Howard Blake; and Section IV incorporates some sentences of his composition.

I have followed with interest some of the work done on Dickinson since the publication of Johnson's edition—including; Charles R. Anderson's justly acclaimed critical study *Emily Dickinson's Poetry; Stairway of Surprise* (1960) and two 'reputation studies' which admirably complement each other, *The Recognition of Emily Dickinson: Selected Criticism since 1890*, edited by Caesar R. Blake and Carlton F. Wells (1964) and *Emily Dickinson: The Critical Revolution*, by Klaus Lubbers (1968). Richard B. Sewall, in the excellent preface to his 1963 "Collection of Critical Essays," rather exaggerates, I think, the significance to criticism of the authoritative edition: at least, the reading of earlier criticism, as assembled by Blake and Wells and by Lubbers, seems to me surprising for the degree of perception and insight with which, despite her own oddities, and the methods of some of her editors, Emily Dickinson and her poems were treated. In his Preface, Mr. Lubbers appositely quotes René Wellek's 'perspectivist' statement that the "total meaning" of a literary work of art is "the result of a process of accretion"—i.e., the history of its criticism by many readers in many ages. Emily Dickinson's poetry seems an admirable case of what Lubbers calls "collective criticism"—what I would prefer to call collaborative criticism.

In the original form of my essay, I commented on Emily Dickinson's at once simplistic and elaborate punctuation of her poems. Like the other critics who reviewed Johnson's edition (all of them accustomed to reading her in regularized texts), I felt initial block and irritation at the literally reproduced text, finding little intelligible and consistent method in Emily's "notation," as Blackmur calls it. My first reaction to E. D.'s 'notation' was to suggest that readers' texts should have all punctuation removed except the full stop (an idea I still think not absurd); but I grant that such a procedure would remove the evidence of the fussing about discriminations which (even though one doesn't attempt precisely to follow them) is an essential characteristic of our poet; and I should like here to register that after having become accustomed to it, I can now read the poems in their 'new' notation as painlessly at least as I do the poems of Hopkins—the more conscious, though the more unintelligible, 'notation' of which I have learned to disregard.

The theoretical and methodical aspects of editing the poems of a poet who did not prepare her own work for publication have been studied in a recent book, at once patient and brilliant, R. W. Franklin's *The Editing of Emily Dickinson: A Reconsideration* (1967). In an important final section of Chapter V, "Criticism and Editing," Franklin writes, "Academically raised in an era that believes in criticism divorced from authorial intention, we face a quandary with the Dickinson texts."

The Marvels of M. R. James, Antiquary

The essays on M. R. James and A. C. Benson, though recently written, go back to interests of the 1940's—interests not initially biographical. It was long after I read James's stories that I became curious to discover what manner of man wrote them. Benson's *From a College Window* was put into my hands when I was about to leave for an American college. In both essays, as I wrote them, the 'advantages' with which these two Edwardian dons were endowed—as sons of Anglican priests, as Etonians and Cantabrigians, as King's College men—obviously engaged me: Theirs was ever a closed and esoteric world; and now it presumably no longer exists in its then structure.

The sources for Dr. James's biography are his own *Eton and King's: Recollections Mostly Trivial* (1926), the Obituary in the London *Times*, June 13, 1936 (cf. also "Appreciations," *ibid.*, June 15), and *A Memoir of Montague Rhodes James*, by S. G. Lubbock (which is followed by a list of his publications, by A. F. Scholfield, 1939). Then there is a delightful volume of his letters (*Letters to a Friend*, edited and with preface by their recipient, Gwendolyn McBride, 1956), containing many interesting allusions to James's reading. There is an easily recognizable portrait of James as "my friend Perry," in *From a College Window* (1906) by A. C. Benson, his schoolfellow at Temple Grove and Eton.

As for comment on Dr. James's ghost stories: There is brief mention of them in Devendra F. Varma's *The Gothic Flame: Being a History of the Gothic Novel in England: Its Origins, Efflorescence, Disintegration, and Residuary Influences* (1957), a rich repository of information and of insight, preceded by Sir Herbert Read's Foreword and an important Introduction by Miss J. M. S. Tompkins. James is mentioned also, and quoted, by the Reverend Montague Summers in his

The Gothic Quest (1938) and in the valuable Introduction to his *Supernatural Omnibus* (1931). The latter Introduction, the best historical and bibliographical piece on the English ghost story I know, repeatedly refers to Dr. James as "the greatest of modern exponents of the supernatural in fiction." Summers (1880–1948), published also a *History of Witchcraft* (presumably the one alluded to in James's "Casting the Runes") and books on the vampire and the werewolf and the Gothic novel. The strange story of this firm believer in ghosts and witches has been told with remarkable skill and taste by Joseph Jerome (*Montague Summers, A Memoir*, 1965).

For "the rules of folklore," I am chiefly indebted to Edwin S. Hartland, *English Fairy and Other Folk Tales* . . . (1890), Alexander H. Krappe, *The Science of Folklore* (1930), and Ernest Jones, *On the Nightmare* (1931).

On Le Fanu, I recommend S. M. Ellis' *Wilkie Collins, Le Fanu and Others* (1931) and the edition of *Green Tea and Other Ghost Stories* published by Arkham House (1945). The informative Foreword to the latter quotes the high praise James gives Le Fanu in his Preface to *Madam Crowl's Ghost and Other Tales of Mystery* (1923); the editor, August Derleth, asserts that America has never had "the ready public for supernatural tales which England has had," and names the two traditions as those of Le Fanu and Poe.

The *Ghostly Tales of Henry James* (1963) has an excellent introduction by Leon Edel, its editor.

Two readily accessible, relevant anthologies are Summers' *A Supernatural Omnibus* (1931) and the Random House (and Modern Library) *Great Tales of Terror and the Supernatural* (ed. H. A. Wise and P. Fraser, 1944), which differentiates the two 'kinds' linked in the title, and includes, as in the second, stories by Henry James as well as M. R. and E. F. Benson, Algernon Blackwood, and H. P. Lovecraft.

For a counterstatement to my 'appreciation' of James's stories, I refer the reader to Edmund Wilson's "A Treatise on Tales of Terror," *Classics and Commercials* . . . (1962), an essay-review of *Great Tales of Terror and the Supernatural*.

A. C. Benson and His Friends

The biographical information in this essay comes from three sources: A Note for American readers prefaced to *Memoirs and Friends* (1924) by Benson himself; Lubbock's parts of Benson's Diary (1926), especially pp. 28–46; and *A. C. Benson as Seen by Some Friends*, ed. by E. H. Ryle (1926). The chief contributors to the memorial "symposium" were Dr. Montague James ("Reminiscences," chiefly of Benson's boyhood and youth), Hugh Macnaghten ("The Eton Master"), Stephen Gaselee (on Benson at Magdalene), Geoffrey Madan (one of Benson's younger and later friends), Lubbock ("The Author of His Books"), and the Reverend Hon. Edward Lyttleton, D.D. (the most outspokenly 'critical' of the Friends, writing on Benson's "Training and Temperament").

The Friends who published the symposium seemingly contemplated, as a further corrective to the misleading impression of him given by his popular books, a selection from Benson's letters. Several of the contributors mention them with praise; and Lubbock ends "The Author of His Books" with the remark, "perhaps, after all, his best writing was not in any of his books, but in his letters," which may not "irretrievably" be lost. However, no such volume of *Selected Letters* has appeared.

Lubbock is the authority for the statement that Benson published about fifty books (*Diary*, 299). No complete bibliography exists, so far as I know: partial publication lists are given in both the *Diary* and Ryle's symposium. Many of the books were issued in uniform gray-green binding by Smith, Elder and Co. *The Memoirs of Arthur Hamilton*, anonymously published in 1886—Benson's earliest book, a half-autobiographical 'Imaginary Portrait'—was reissued under his name in 1907 (by Mitchell Kennerley).

Benson's manuscript *Diary* (180 small volumes) is now kept, together with other papers of his, in the Archives of

Magdalene College; the sealed boxes may not be opened before 1975.

The chronicle of how James's *William Wetmore Story and His Friends* came to be written has now become available in Leon Edel's *Henry James; The Treacherous Years* (1969), 198–99. The financial arrangements, including an advance payment of 250 pounds, were made not directly with the importunate Storys but with William Blackmore of Edinburgh, who had published Story's verses, plays, and essays. Benson's friendship with James is also discussed in *The Treacherous Years*, 88–89 and 245–48.

On Lubbock's friendship with Benson and his editing of Benson's *Diary*, I am glad to cite, and to recommend, Charles W. Mayer's "Percy Lubbock: Disciple of Henry James," a Michigan dissertation directed by Professor Lyall Powers and as yet unpublished, which reached me only after I had written my essay. Especially relevant are Mayer's pages 9–10 and 41–42; but Chapters I and II (the former on Lubbock's friendships and the latter on his biographies and 'portraits') are illuminating and just. Mayer puts Lubbock's attitude toward Benson in a perspective partially corrective of mine by showing with what rigor this meticulous critic and biographer treated the careers of such other writer-friends of his as Mary Cholmondeley, George Calderon, and even Edith Wharton (*The Portrait of Edith Wharton*, published in 1947, found Mrs. Wharton to fall short of the artist's true standards and lavishly praised but one of her novels, *The Reef*). Lubbock cherished his friends as persons, but he could not tolerate amateur writing; and, by comparison with the Master, James, all his other friends seemed insufficiently dedicated and consummate.

Between Benson and T. S. Eliot there are three curious links. In his 1930 essay, "Arnold and Pater," Eliot quotes from "Dr. Benson's" *Pater* in the 'English Men of Letters Series.' Then the late Morton Zabel discovered that Eliot's opening lines in "Gerontion," with their images of "an old man in a dry month/Being read to by a boy, waiting for rain," were adapted from the opening of the next to last chapter of Benson's *Edward FitzGerald* in the same series. And lastly, I. A. Richards, who was a member of Magdalene College, Cambridge, speaks of lending his copy of Eliot's *Ara Vos Prec* (1919) to Benson, who (with his ecclesiastical background) detected signs of a Catholic trend in "Mr. Eliot's Sunday Morning Service" and, returning the copy, commented, "Watch out! I hear the beat of the capripede hoof" (*Eliot: The Man and His Work*, ed. by Allen Tate, 1966, 6).

Paul Elmer More

Paul Elmer More was an elder acquaintance and correspondent of mine in the late 1920's and early 1930's; in a paragraph on p. 133, I have recorded the impression his person made on me. In 1928 (*Sewanee Review*, XXXVI, 246–50), I reviewed his *Christ the Word* under the heading, "Mr. More Discovers Christianity." The review was that of an arrogant youth who had not read the older man's *Shelburnes* and who judged the book in isolation from More's whole career. In my essay, I have attempted an 'act of reparation.' My essay practices the 'rhetoric of silence' as well as the method of strict statement, and should so be read. I do not share the view of his friend Babbitt and others that More excelled as a stylist: his style is neither liturgical enough on the one hand nor characteristic-expressive on the other; I prefer Babbitt's style in *Literature and the American College* and *The Masters of French Criticism*. And I do not consider More a critic's critic or a philosopher's philosopher—a great original force. But I do consider him something like a 'representative man,' an exemplary humanist, impressive by virtue of his character of intellect.

Arthur Hazard Dakin's *A Paul Elmer More Miscellany* (1950) contains a full bibliography of More's published writings and of writings about him. More's chief works, now all out of print, are the *Shelburne Essays*, in eleven volumes, 1904–21, and *The Greek Tradition*, in four volumes and two complementary volumes, 1917–31. His most personal and most popular books are *The Sceptical Approach to Religion* (1934) and *Pages from an Oxford Diary* (1937).

Dakin's *Paul Elmer More* (1960) is an extraordinarily careful and full biography, which copiously quotes More's letters, and gives what, as his biographer says, "even those closest to him . . . had little means of obtaining[,] a reasonably full and intimate account of his personality." And Francis X. Duggan's *Paul Elmer More* (1966, a volume in Twayne's 'United States Authors Series') can be recommended as a remarkably intelligent, accurate, and just interpretation and estimate of More's work; it should be better known.

Paul Elmer More's Shelburne Essays on American Literature, selected and edited by Daniel Aaron (1963), makes available essays (long out of print) which gain considerably by being assembled. Aaron's introduction illuminatingly analyzes More's pioneer and thoroughly independent criticism of American, chiefly New England, literature.

Historical interpretations of More's period, especially studies of movements of which he was in some sense a part, bear witness to his being, among other things, an intersection of many intellectual interests. He will be found treated in books on the New Humanist Movement of the early 1930's (by Louis J. A. Mercier, Folke Leander, and G. R. Elliott), on the Conservative tradition in America (by Russell Kirk, Clinton Rossiter, and Allen Guttman), in histories of American and modern American criticism (by Bernard Smith, M. D. Zabel, and Walter Sutton). William D. Geoghegan considers More in *Platonism in Recent Religious Thought* (1958); and René Wellek is illuminating on More's Platonism and his relation to Emerson in an essay contributed to *Transcendentalism and Its Legacy* (ed. by Myron Simon and T. H. Parsons, 1966). In essays by Edmund Wilson (*The Triple Thinkers*), Alfred Kazin (*On Native Grounds*), and Daniel Aaron (*op.cit.*), one sees More emerging as an honorable specimen of the 'engaged' critic, whose work gains in seriousness, weight, and even durability by his commitment to more than aesthetic values.

It has seemed unwise, in the context of my book of 'literary' essays, to extend to More's philosophical and theological work the relative fullness of analysis I have given to his criticism. A brief but sound essay on "Paul Elmer More as a Theologian" has been written by the Reverend W. Norman Pittenger; it will be found as Chapter 14 of Pittenger's *Theology and Reality* . . . (1955).

The connection, the relation, between More in his theological period and T. S. Eliot in his later, his postconversion, period, was important corroboration for both. On February 5, 1937, the *Princeton Alumni Weekly* printed Eliot's tribute to More (I should add that Dakin, who reprints parts of it, quotes also from a letter of Eliot's to Professor Thorp which adds some reservations honorably compatible with the published eulogy).

The Paul Elmer More papers, at the Princeton University Library, include both sides of the correspondence between More and Eliot.

Continuity and Coherence in the Criticism of T. S. Eliot

Eliot's critical writing is as close as his poetry; in kind it is as economical. An essay of ten or twelve pages says as much as many another man's book. It offers the 'heads' of a discourse, the 'topic sentences,' a few examples (some lines of verse, some names), and leaves 'development' to the reader.

An Eliot essay offers no final sentence or paragraph of summary and defies the summary-making of others. His meaning is more or less coterminous with his essay. He is always thinking—as he writes, as well as before; and, in consequence, it is of no profit to try to 'speed-read' him.

To write on Eliot's criticism requires the establishment of the right distance from the texts upon which interpretation must be based. Come too close to them, as the exegetical scholar is likely to do, and you will get a collection of distinctions and discriminations each so firmly phrased as to sound prescriptive, and you will be left with the never-ending business of adjusting these distinctions to each other. On the other hand, read intensely and copiously, and you are likely not to remember more than isolated sentences or paragraphs which coincided, or collided with, your own prejudices, either toward Eliot or on the topics he has been pondering. Again: too attentive to Eliot, too respectful and docile, and you get drawn into his orbit; too detached and impatient, or too hostile, and you make of him a strawman, a target, or an enemy. I have been a sympathetic reader of Eliot's criticism since his first prose book, *The Sacred Wood* (1920), and coming to it after having studied with Irving Babbitt at Harvard and already an Anglican, I owe so much to Eliot's criticism, itself partially taking off from Babbitt's 'Humanism,' that I have found this matter of the 'right distance' as difficult as rewarding to establish.

The first section of my present essay was written, as internal evidence shows, not long after 1939. Finding it among my papers, ready for publication, but as yet unpublished, I contributed it to Allen Tate's memorial volume, *T.S. Eliot: The Man and His Work* (*Sewanee Review*, 1966; published in book form by the Delacorte Press). In this piece, entitled "Continuity in T.S. Eliot's Literary Criticism," I followed Section I with some new pages on Eliot's 1957 *On Poetry and the Poets*. On rereading it, I found my later sections, as there printed, unsatisfactory. What now follows Section I is new, written in 1969, after I had reread Eliot's prose and as much of the 'criticism of his criticism' and other 'collateral literature' as, without losing my own critical balance, I could manage.

Section I (my early essay) has seemed to me worth retaining, as presenting a relatively coherent (as well as almost entirely sympathetic) view of Eliot's criticism. The rest of the essay has, however, more detachment. In establishing this, I was helped by Eliot's critics, and especially those highly critical of his criticism (e.g., Leavis, Ransom, and Winters). The bibliography with which this note ends includes only essays which I have used with profit.

M. C. Bradbrook, "Eliot's Critical Method," in *Eliot: A Study of His Writings by Several Hands*, ed. B. Rajan (1947).

Connections

Northrup Frye, *T. S. Eliot* (1963). Chaps 1 and 2 ("Antique Drum" and "Dialect of the Tribe").

David A. Huisman, "An Extra-Human Measure: T.S. Eliot and the Theological Evaluation of Literature." (Unpublished University of Michigan dissertation, 1967.)

Stanley Hyman, "T.S. Eliot and Tradition in Criticism," *The Armed Vision: A Study in the Methods of Modern Literary Criticism* (1948).

F. R. Leavis, "T.S. Eliot as a Critic," *Anna Karenina and Other Essays* (1967, first published 1958).

Fei-Pai Lu, *T.S. Eliot: The Dialectical Structure of His Theory of Poetry* (1966).

Mario Praz, "T.S. Eliot as a Critic," *Sewanee Review*, 1966.

Philip Rahv, "Eliot's Achievement," *New York Review of Books*, March 3, 1966.

J. C. Ransom, "T.S. Eliot: The Historical Critic," *The New Criticism*, 1941.

René Wellek, "The Criticism of T.S. Eliot," *Sewanee Review*, Summer 1956.

Raymond Williams, "T. S. Eliot," *Culture and Society, 1780–1950* (1958). (A discussion of *The Idea of a Christian Society* and *Notes for a Definition of Culture*.)

Yvor Winters, "T.S. Eliot, or the Illusion of Reaction," *In Defense of Reason* (1947).